REASONS
FOR
BELIEVING

REASONS FOR BELIEVING

A Seeker's Guide to Christianity

Frank Harber

New Leaf Press

First printing: April 1998
Fourth printing: July 2002

ISBN: 0-89221-422-8
Library of Congress Catalog Number: 98-66301

Cover design: Lee Fredrickson

All Scripture quotations are from the New King James
Version of the Bible.

Printed in the United States of America

Please visit our website for other great titles:
www.newleafpress.net

For information regarding author interviews, please con-
tact the publicity department at (870) 438-5288.

DEDICATION

This book is dedicated to
Becky, Graham, Gabrielle,
Rick, Kaye,
Danny, Zack, Savanna —
my family.

TABLE OF CONTENTS

Why not give Christianity a trial? The question seems a hopeless one after 2,000 years of resolute adherence to the old cry of "Not this man, but Barabbas. . . ." "This man" has not been a failure yet, for nobody has ever been sane enough to try his way.

George Bernard Shaw

Preface
Androcles and the Lion

INTRODUCTION

It is no accident that you are reading this book! Reading this book can be a major turning point in your life. The information in this book contains much of the factual evidence found during my personal search for the truth. I pray this book will provide you with many of the answers for which you have been looking.

The decision to search for ultimate truth is a free choice. Many people live full lives and never discover the truth about God. Perhaps this lies in the fact that one needs to seek after God to find Him (Jer. 29:13). God never forces himself upon people. God's revelation of truth is such that it never compels non-seekers against their will.

This book is for honest seekers who want to know the truth about God. An honest seeker is someone who is willing to take an objective look at the evidence and make a decision. Jesus gave His word that anyone who conducts an honest search for the truth shall find the answers:

> Ask, and it will be given to you; seek, and you will find; knock, and it will be

opened to you. For everyone who asks receives, and he who seeks finds, and to him who knocks it will be opened (Matt. 7:7-8).

The process of seeking after God is laden with pitfalls. All of us have pre-suppositions and bias which affect the way that we view evidence. There are four major pitfalls you should be aware of when you are seeking God.

First, you have a moral bias.

The number one reason people reject Jesus is the love of sin. Sin is simply rebellion against God. Sin separates humankind from God. The Bible teaches that sin can be temporarily pleasurable and fun (Heb. 11:25).

The key word is "temporarily" because sin eventually brings forth death (Rom. 6:23). Jesus' message was that sin is serious and leads to eternal separation from God. Jesus said it was because of this message that the world would hate Him (John 7:7).

This hatred for Jesus' message led to several stages. At first people tolerated the message of Jesus, but eventually it led to a desire to eliminate Jesus through crucifixion. The rejection of truth always leads to the desire to eliminate the truth — man kills God!

In your search, the temptation will be to quit searching once you begin to uncover the evidence. The reason that you will want to do this is that you will find that becoming a Christian is really not an "intellectual" issue as much as it is a "willingness" issue. Your main problem is not in your "head," it's in your "heart."

You have a sin problem. You will find it a struggle to be willing to repent of your sin and turn your life over to Christ. You will grope for intellectual excuses why you won't repent. So be aware that the love of sin will certainly color your search. Be honest about this fact and you will do well.

Second, inaccurate evidence leads to wrong conclusions.

One of the greatest barriers to becoming a Christian is that many skeptics do not study the right evidence. It is very important to look at the best possible evidence.

Many non-Christians have made up their minds about Christianity based upon hearsay information. Hearsay information is not admissible in a court of law and should not be used in making a determination about something as important as Christianity.

Even in Jesus' day, He was faced with inaccurate statements made about himself. Some of Jesus' skeptics charged that it was impossible that he could be the Christ since He was from Galilee and the Christ would be from Bethlehem (John 7:41-42). However, if these skeptics had checked their facts more closely, they would have discovered that Jesus was indeed born in Bethlehem. The place of Jesus' birth is now so well-known that one chuckles when the story of these allegations are made.

Most non-Christians would truly be surprised if they would only study the evidence for themselves. I suspect that most people don't actually reject Jesus as much as they reject a false image of Jesus.

Most non-Christians have not rejected

Christianity on intellectual grounds. Most people never take the time to take a detailed look at the evidence. However, some of Christianity's greatest champions were former skeptics who sought to discredit Christianity and were compelled to believe once they viewed the evidence. If you will only examine the evidence for yourself, you will be surprised at what you will find.

Open-mindedness, not tolerance, is required of the search.

Perhaps the greatest virtue esteemed in secular society today is tolerance. Society frowns upon those who would make value judgments about the beliefs and morals of others. Some hold that no one's truth or values should be held to be superior to anyone else's.

Relativism means what is true for you is not necessarily true for me. Relativism is a particularly appealing position when dealing with religion. This has led some to assert that all religions are equally valid. How can all the religions of the world all be true when they all contradict each other?

Christianity differs from many religions in the fact that it claims to have unique ownership of truth. This is a staggering claim. What if this claim is true? What are the implications? Christianity does not claim to be one of many truths; it claims to be *the* truth. If you are truly an open-minded person, you must take this claim very seriously. You must determine if there is any evidence which validates that Christianity is indeed the truth.

Last, Christianity requires faith.

Christianity contains ample evidence to persuade any open-minded seeker but does not always persuade the closed-minded skeptic. Without a doubt, Christianity requires faith. The step of faith is the initial requirement to becoming a Christian (Eph. 2:8-9). Hebrews 11:6 states, "Without faith it is impossible to please Him, for he who comes to God must believe that He is, and that He is a rewarder of those who diligently seek Him."

Christianity does not require "unrealistic faith" but a "reasonable faith." Faith is based on a solid foundation of evidence. Nonetheless, some faith is required. This is a difficult proposition for some who seek absolute proof before they will make a faith commitment. The Bible promises faith produces assurance. Many seekers delay exercising faith because they seek absolute assurance before they will make a faith commitment. But God's promise of assurance must be preceded by faith.

Many seekers wish to eradicate all doubts before they will become Christians. If taken too far, this philosophy can produce a dangerous spiritual position. Delaying a faith decision is spiritually perilous in light of the fact that it can become a permanent position.

Becoming a Christian does not mean that all doubts and questions cease. I've learned more about God since I became a Christian than I could have ever dreamed. Every day, with new spiritual insights and archeological and scientific discoveries, even more of my questions are answered and my faith in God is strengthened.

Always remember that where faith is required, doubt is possible. It never surprises me when I meet skeptics of the Christian faith. God's requirement of faith opens the door for rejection of God. Rejection of God is thus often expressed in the language of doubt.

God has ordered His universe such that an honest seeker can easily find the truth. In a world of faith the truth can easily remain hidden to those who don't wish to see. It is the pre-supposition of this book that honest seekers can truly find God. In fact, as you read this book, you will discover in your search for God that He has already been searching for you. Jesus is the true seeker (Luke 19:10).

Before you read the remainder of this book, ask yourself this question, "Am I an honest seeker?" Are you willing to follow the evidence wherever it may lead you? If you are truly sincere in your search, you will find the truth.

Before you begin the first chapter, I want to ask you to do what I did before I began my search. I specifically asked Christ to fulfill His promise that all who seek Him will find Him. I prayed what is called the "seekers prayer." Please find the courage and honesty to also pray this prayer before you read this book:

Dear God,

I am not sure if You exist or not, but I want to find out. If You are there, I want You to know that I am honestly going to seek You and wish to hold You to your promise that all honest seekers will be rewarded. I want to know the truth no matter what. I promise that if You reveal to me that You are real, I will commit my life to You and become a Christian. If You really exist, help me in my search and keep me from turning back until I find the truth. Amen.

If you just prayed that prayer, you will not regret this *important* first step in finding God. The evidence that you are about to read can change your life forever.

For the scientist who has lived by his faith in the power of reason, the story ends like a bad dream. He has scaled the mountains of ignorance; he is about to conquer the highest peak; as he pulls himself over the final rock, he is greeted by a band of theologians who have been sitting there for centuries.

Dr. Robert Jastrow

Founder of NASA's Institute
for Space Studies

1

GOD EXISTS

I n 1859, Charles Darwin's *Origin of Species* was published. In this work, Darwin set forth the theory of natural selection. His theory centered around the concept of the "survival of the fittest." He theorized that organisms engaged in a struggle for survival; the organisms which are able to survive pass on their superior survival attributes to their offspring in the form of new and improved genes. The most striking part of his theory was the assertion that modern animals came into existence through natural processes. This theory came to be labeled as "evolution."

Prior to 1859, the dominant population maintained that God had created the universe. By the end of the Scopes trial, evolution was a universally accepted fact. Belief in God was associated with pre-scientific myths. The implications of evolution were applied in other areas of knowledge such as the social sciences, humanities, business, and politics. John Dewey, the former biologist from Yale, designed the public schools on these very premises. Soon even religion was explained in terms of evolution, as Christianity was compromised by those eager to maintain their faith and a belief in evolution.

As a major result of the acceptance of the theory of evolution, many people lost their faith in God. Once a professing Christian, Darwin abandoned his faith in light of his acceptance of evolution. The connection of the acceptance of evolution with the loss of faith is well-established. In fact, the acceptance of the theory of evolution is the number one cause of the loss of religious faith.[1] This is primarily because the theory of evolution runs counter to a supernatural creation. To introduce supernaturalism at any point is to violate the evolutionary theory.

Darwin wrote: "I would give absolutely nothing for the theory of natural selection if it requires miraculous additions at any one stage of descent."[2] The Bible does not support a theory of biblical evolution but clearly teaches special creation. Thus, it is of little wonder why many who have accepted evolution as true have abandoned their faith in God.

Surprisingly, the theory of evolution remains unproven. In fact, the evidence of science provides facts which prove evolution is not true at all. To begin, there are several major flaws in evolution. In

Darwin's *The Origin of the Species*, he never gave one single example of any new species of plants or animals arising from natural selection. No scientist can produce any substantial evidence that evolution has taken place in the past nor are there any examples that it is taking place today.

There are many examples of microevolution (changes within species) but none for macroevolution (the general theory of evolution sometimes called the "molecules to man" theory). There has not been one single documented example of any organism evolving into a more complex kind of new species. The past and present evidence indicate "extinction," not "evolution," has prevailed.

Another major flaw in the theory of evolution is that it cannot account for the origin of life. There has been much misunderstanding in the media that life has been synthesized from non-living chemicals in the laboratory. This is not so. Even if scientists were able to produce life, this would not prove that a non-living substance created life. It would prove the opposite, demonstrating that it took great effort for intelligent beings to "reproduce" what already existed. This would merely demonstrate that it takes intelligence to create!

Evolutionists have theorized that what intelligent humanity is unable to accomplish with high tech equipment, somehow happened by chance. Henry Morris observes, "Thus the evolutionist has to resort to an explanation in terms of an imaginary atmosphere which no longer exists, an imaginary ocean composition which no longer exists, and hypothetical processes which no longer exist, to explain the evolution of primitive organisms which no longer exist: Whatever philosophic or religious value such speculations might have, they are certainly not scientific."[3]

Modern research has shown that natural selection is not capable of creating anything new. Darwin was unaware of the DNA/RNA genetic system within each organism. We now understand that natural selection does not produce new genes; it only selects among pre-existing characteristics. Thus, natural selection does not deal with "new" types but with types already in existence.

To overcome the genetic barriers in evolution, mutations have been proposed as the process by which new genetic material was generated for the origin of new species. But, mutations are harmful. No beneficial mutation has ever been observed. Many laboratory experiments have been used to induce mutations by chemicals, radiations, and other influences, but all have resulted in deterioration. Evolutionists have speculated that somewhere in the past beneficial mutations occurred, but even if mutations were helpful, they would only deal with changes in existing characteristics. New functioning organs would have to be produced for evolution to occur. For a simple organism to develop a mutation which could create an eye is unthinkable. It is difficult to comprehend how thousands of random mutations could coincide to make such a miracle possible, yet thousands and thousands of such miraculous mutations are needed to make evolution possible.

Evolution continues to be promoted as a fact of

science, not because of the evidence, but because the alternative of divine creation is not optional in the mind of many. Evolution has become a form of mythology in which one has to believe a magical explanation for the origin of life. To challenge this well-established theory is to find oneself being viewed as unscientific.

Evolution is not based on science as much as it is based on philosophy. Evolution, a materialistic philosophy, has a prejudice toward the supernatural and twists scientific facts to fit its own interpretation. Evolution has come to resemble a fairy tale without any factual basis. To believe the theory of evolution requires a great deal of faith, which requires belief in many illogical and impossible scenarios. Holding to such an unproven theory requires the imagination of "Alice in Wonderland" who laughed at the contradictory logic of the Red Queen: "There's no use trying," she said. "One can't believe impossible things." "I dare say you haven't had much practice," said the Queen. "When I was your age I did it for half an hour a day. Why sometimes I've believed as many as six impossible things before breakfast."[4] In spite of the evidence, evolution is dogmatically taught as fact.

In truth, far more evidence supports the theory of creation than the theory of evolution. Belief in God is not a superstitious faith in an invisible nothing. The Christian faith is built upon solid scientific and historical evidence.

Most non-believers reject God not because they have examined the evidence, but because of their own preconceived ideas. Most who argue against God have never had the intellectual integrity to examine the historical evidence for Christianity (which is readily available) in order to reject the evidence.

The Bible is not the only source of knowledge that gives evidence of the existence of God. The sources of empirical knowledge available abound with convincing evidence which points to the existence of God.

EVIDENCE FROM PHYSICS

Perhaps the greatest blow to the theory of evolution is the first and second laws of thermodynamics. These laws are proven scientific laws and are accepted by all reputable scientists.

The First Law of Thermodynamics

The first law of thermodynamics is referred to as the Law of Energy Conservation, holding that the amount of mass and energy is constant. Mass and energy are interchangeable but neither can be created or destroyed. Because none of the tremendous energy now available is presently being created, it is impossible that the present universe could have created itself. Because the present natural processes cannot create energy, energy had to have been created by an agency outside the scope of the present universe.

The Second Law of Thermodynamics

The second law of thermodynamics is perhaps the most devastating evidence against evolution. The second law is referred to as the Law of Energy

Decay or Law of Entropy. The second law holds that all the available energy in the universe is decreasing. Material things in the universe age, wear out, decay, and die. The universe is proceeding downward from order to disorder; consequently, the universe will eventually die of heat-death as the molecules in the universe will move into a random pattern incapable of being used again (see Isa. 51:6). Our universe is running out of usable fuel. For example, the moment a star is born it begins to use up massive amounts of hydrogen. Because there is a limited supply of hydrogen and some still exists, the universe could not be eternal.

Because the universe is dying, if time were stretched back infinitely, the universe would have already run down. Thus, the universe had to have had a beginning. Evolution requires that millions of natural processes evolved upward and became more complex. Such a theory which requires billions of years and multiple violations of the second law of thermodynamics is statistically improbable. Many noted scientists hold that when the laws of thermodynamics are properly understood, they are enough to refute the theory of evolution.[5] Because the created universe could not create itself, there must have been a Creator.

EVIDENCE FROM BIOLOGY

The universe exhibits an incredible design and purposeful order. The universe displays numerous complex and remarkable organisms that defy any naturalistic explanation. Earth is the home of wondrous creatures such as the archerfish which can shoot water 15 feet into the air and strike an insect. The universe is perfectly designed for supporting intelligent life forms.

Because the universe is so intricately designed, it is highly improbable it could have originated by accident. This world contains 11 million different kinds of species. Each of these represents an amazing design of engineering and life. Yet, man, in all of his intelligence, is not even able to create one new species. Pollster George Gallup once commented that the existence of God was statistically provable: "Take the human body alone — the chance that all the functions of the individual could just happen, is a statistical monstrosity."[6]

Every intelligent design indicates a designer. The greater the design, the greater the designer. The complex structure of the universe declares that there had to have been a great Architect. An accident could not have formed our great universe. Beavers who construct small pond dams could never construct a dam comparable to Hoover Dam. There is a great intelligence behind nature. We pay homage to this concept whenever we use the term "Mother Nature," in referring to the intelligence behind nature. Almost all of the complex discoveries of modern science, such as electrical, mechanical, acoustical, and optical phenomena, are already present in nature. Consider the sonar of porpoises, the frequency-modulated radar of bats, and the aerodynamics of the hummingbird. Reason tells us that there must be a great Designer who has designed and continually maintains our universe. Consider the following biological evidence.

The Brain

The brain weighs just over three pounds but can do what tons of electrical and electronic equipment cannot. It contains up to 15 billion neurons, each a living unit within itself. Over 100 thousand billion (10^{14}) electrical connections are present which is more than "all the electrical connections in all the electrical appliances in the world."[7] Every cubic inch contains a minimum of 100 million nerve cells interconnected by 10 thousand miles of fibers to other nerve cells in the brain.[8] Michael Denton comments:

> Even if only one-hundredth of the connections in the brain were specifically organized, this would represent a system containing a much greater number of specific connections than the entire communications network on earth. Because of the vast number of unique adaptive connections, to assemble an object remotely resembling the brain would take an eternity even applying the most sophisticated engineering techniques.[9]

Could such sophisticated design and engineering have occurred by accident?

The Eye

The human eye contains 130,000,000 light sensitive rods and cones which generate photochemical reactions that convert light into electrical impulses.[10] An incredible one billion such impulses are transmitted to the brain every second.[11] The eye can make over 100 thousand separate motions and, when confronted with darkness, can increase its ability to see 100 thousand times.[12] It comes complete with automatic aiming, automatic focusing, and automatic maintenance during one's sleep. To think that thousands of chance mutations accidentally formed such a structure is impossible. Also within the evolutionary framework, the eye would have needed to evolve several times in the different kinds of species, such as squids and arthropods. The human eye is so sophisticated that scientists still do not fully understand it. Such an intelligent design points to a Designer.

The Cell

The cell, which was thought to be of very simple design in Darwin's day, is now known to be highly complex. A single bacteria cell is only 1/1000 of a millimeter and yet its complexity is comparable to a chemical factory. Functions and tasks are carried out by the thousands. The cell has energy generators, defensive systems, transport systems, food factories, protective barriers, waste removal structures, and communicational processes both inside and outside its own cell limits. Human beings have up to 100 billion of these self-contained cities.[13] The complex molecules within even one cell contain a vast information content so great that evolution could not be possible.

EVIDENCE FROM BIOCHEMISTRY

Biochemistry is the chemistry of living systems. This field is important to the study of the origin of life. In 1938 the Russian chemist O. I. Oparin proposed that the first forms of life emerged from "a primordial soup of complex chemicals through reactions with electrical discharges under an assumed reducing [no-oxygen] primeral atmosphere."[14] Life was said to have originated from chance via complex chemicals, but then came the advent of the electron microscope and as the unseen level became visible, a new story was told.

The Law of Biogenesis

Evolution requires that spontaneous generation (life coming from non-living matter) must have occurred. But not one case of spontaneous generation has ever been observed. All scientific observations point to the fact that life only comes from life. This scientific law is referred to as the Law of Biogenesis. Hence, to get life you need life.

Telonomy

The field of chemistry has verified that there is a fundamental difference between living and non-living things. The difference found in living things is referred to as telonomy. Telonomy is the information that is contained within a living organism. It refers to design and order which can be utilized by "energy and matter to produce complexity."[15] Telonomy is illustrated in comparing the difference between a dead stick and a live tree. Telonomy utilizes nutrients and energy from the sun to increase its order; whereas, the energy of the sun upon the dead stick only speeds up its decay process. For spontaneous generation to occur, the forces of chemicals and energy would have only worked if the designed and coded information was already present. This is why creation is the only logical explanation. It takes intelligence to create!

EVIDENCE FROM GENETICS

All forms of life are dependent upon DNA (deoxyribonucleic acid) molecules. DNA programs the characteristics of each organism. It determines the height, hair color, skeletal arrangement of 206 bones, 600 muscles, 10,000 auditory nerve fibers, 2 million optic nerve fibers, 100 billion nerve cells, and 400 billion feet of blood vessels and capillaries.[16] This genetic material which controls the physical processes of life is coded information. This information is accompanied by elaborate transmission and duplication systems necessary for the continuation of life.

DNA functions according to programmed information. No natural process has ever been observed that has been able to produce a program. A program is a series of steps taken to accomplish a goal. To illustrate, a computer program is an example of a program. However, "computer scientists have demonstrated that information does not and cannot arise spontaneously."[17] Thus, DNA could have only been formed by intelligence.

The ability of DNA to store information is incredible. The amount of information in DNA needed to design every organism that ever existed could be held in less than a teaspoon, and there would still be enough room to hold the information contained in every book ever written.[18] Even a single amoeba's DNA has enough information storage capacity to contain the information stored in a thousand sets of encyclopedias.[19] If the 46 segments of DNA in one human cell were stretched out, it would be about seven feet long.[20] And if all the DNA of the 100,000,000,000,000 cells of the body were stretched out, it would stretch from the earth to the moon more than 500,000 times.[21] Could such an elaborate, coded, complex program have originated by an accident? Such belief requires faith far greater than those who believe in creation.

EVIDENCE FROM MATHEMATICS

Evolutionists argue that with enough time, even the most improbable events become probable. Evolution requires billions of years for life to have evolved by chance; however, evolution is still impossible in light of the principles of probability.

The odds of a one-celled animal emerging by chance is one in 10^{40000}.[22] The chance of man evolving is one in $10^{2,000,000,000}$.[23] These odds are staggering considering that five billion years is only 10^{17} seconds and the visible universe has less than 10^{80} atoms in it.[24] The odds of life emerging by chance are even more incredible when it is known, according to Borel's single law of chance, that anything beyond 1 in 10^{50} is "impossible." Sir Fred Hoyle equates the chances of the universe happening by chance with that of a tornado blowing through a junkyard containing the parts of a 747 and accidentally assembling the parts, making it ready for flight.[25] The universe being created by chance is not a true scientific option. Webster defines chance as "something that happens as the result of unknown or unconsidered forces." We sometimes think of flipping a coin as chance, but is it? What makes a coin come up heads or tails? Actually a certain amount of speed and pressure rotates the coin. This, combined with the density of the air, will produce a specific number of revolutions. Once all these facts are known, we know "exactly" why the coin turned up heads or tails. Chance was not the cause. Chance is a non-entity with no power or reality; and if the chances of evolution are one in 10^{1000}, the chance of creation would be far greater than 99.9, making creation infinitely probable. If these two explanations are the only alternatives, then one can say with great certainty that creation occurred!

EVIDENCE FROM PALEONTOLOGY

Paleontology is the scientific study of fossils. The fossil record has often been cited as one of the main evidences for evolution. According to the general theory of evolution, the basic progression of life was as such:

1. Non-living matter
2. Protozoans
3. Metazoan invertebrates
4. Vertebrate fishes
5. Amphibians
6. Reptiles
7. Birds
8. Fur-bearing quadrupeds
9. Apes
10. Man.[26]

In Darwin's day a cell was thought to be very simple, but with the advent of powerful microscopes, we know that the likelihood of evolution of single to multiple-cell organisms has been vastly overestimated. If evolution were true, one would expect to find the transitional sequences from one species to another, but in the mile-deep fossil graveyard around the world, there are huge gaps in the fossil record. No transitional fossils have been found. Where are the millions of creatures that should be part-reptile, part-bird, part-ape, and part-human? The term "missing link" is deceiving because for evolution to be true, there should not be one intermediate link but thousands; consequently, the reason no such forms can be found is because such creatures never existed.

The geological record does not reveal the gradual evolution of organisms but sudden appearance of fully developed forms of life. The fossil record indicates that millions of plants and animals have lived and died on earth. The fossil record does not support the evolution of life over many ages but the destruction of life in one age.

A century ago evolutionists promised that these gaps would be filled, but the gaps remain. The study of fossilization has revealed billions and billions of fossils preserved in an abnormal way. Massive fossil graveyards have been uncovered that contain various animals from different climatic areas buried together. Such large scale fossilization does not occur today. When animals die they do not fossilize, they decompose.

The spectacular examples of fossilization point

to a worldwide, hydraulic, aqueous cataclysm. This is consistent with the destruction described by the Genesis flood. This flood explains why fossils from one supposed evolutionary age are found mixed in with fossils from another age.

Evidence in the fossil record is embarrassing to the theory of evolution. The fossil record indicates that creation has occurred.

EVIDENCE FROM ANTHROPOLOGY

According to evolution, humans are the most recent arrival in evolutionary history. Evolutionists hold that man evolved from apes by way of a pre-human form called "hominids." Since this theory has been put forth, scientists have been looking for fossil evidence of ape-men. This assumption has spawned many unscientific approaches which have claimed their fossil ape was the missing link which has led to a series of frauds in the scientific community.

There have been many fossils of true humans and true apes but none of ape-humans. Evolutionists, eager to fill in the genealogical vacuum, have often prematurely publicized evidence which later had to be retracted. The following chart lists the major evidence which has been touted as the missing link.

The common belief of ape-human ancestors does not stem from solid evidence but imaginative depictions by artists. Imaginative reconstruction from such scarce information can be best attributed to a preconditioned evolutionary bias. Thus, the facts do not support the fictitious attempts to find

HOMINID EVIDENCE

DATE	FIND	LOCATION	EVIDENCE	FINDING
1891	Java Man	Java	Skull cap, 3 teeth, thighbone, found with ape bones	Large gibbon
1900	Neanderthal Man	Western Germany	Skeletons with large brain capacities	Completely human
1912	Piltdown Man	Piltdown, England	Faked fossils in a gravel pit	Hoax
1922	Nebraska Man	Nebraska	Tooth	Pig's tooth (Scopes trial evidence)
1928	Peking Man	Peking	Evidence disappeared	Controversial from the beginning
1932	Ramapithecus	India	Teeth and jaw fragment	True ape similar to orangutan
1972	Australo- pithecines	Ethiopia	40% complete skeleton	Extinct ape similar to modern pygmy chimpanzee

ape-humans, but support the biblical evidence that humans were created by God.

EVIDENCE FROM ASTRONOMY

The observable data coming in from the study of astronomy has led astronomers to believe that the universe had a point of origin. Astronomer Edwin Hubble observed that the universe seemed to be expanding in every direction. This led George Gamow to trace the process back to where the universe was compressed into a primordial atom. This atom exploded creating the present universe. This theory is popularly known as the "big-bang theory." Support for the big-bang theory is supported by:

1. An omnidirectional background radiation in the universe discovered in 1965.

2. A "red shift" of light is coming from stars which may mean that the galaxies are rushing outward from a center point.

3. Albert Einstein's extension of his theory of relativity led him to conclude that the universe is simultaneously expanding and decelerating.

However, several problems exist with the big-bang theory. Many astrophysicists do not hold to this theory. Why? Explosions produce disorder, not order. How could such an explosion, which is driving the galaxies apart, "fail to drive all atoms apart before they came together in galaxies?"[27]

Furthermore, such an explosion cannot explain why all the planets and moons do not rotate in the same direction. Six of the 63 moons, along with Venus, Uranus, and Pluto, rotate backwards.[28] Jupiter, Saturn, and Neptune have moons which rotate both directions.[29]

The universe does not resemble the chaotic remains of an explosion. Rather, the universe is a marvel of orderliness. Planet earth exists in a most incredible part of the cosmos which is conducive to life. Earth itself is enveloped with an innumerable group of miraculous coincidences which make life possible. For all the conditions for life to be possible to have been caused by chance assaults one's common sense. Here are but a few of the many amazing coincidences:

The Sun

The sun fits the exact specifications for a life-bearing planet. Only one-fourth of the stars in the universe are bachelor stars. The sun also fits the criteria of being a middle-aged star required for life. It is the perfect distance from the earth — 93 million miles. The surface of the sun is 11,500 degrees Fahrenheit, and its core is over 40 million degrees. This heat travelling 93 million miles is what heats our planet. If 50 degrees more or less average per year reached our planet, life would cease to exist.

The Earth's Rotation

The earth rotates at a speed of over 1,000 miles per hour. Every year this speed is slowed by a fraction of a second.[30] If the earth were to spin at one-tenth less than its present speed, life would be destroyed by searing heat during the day and devastating freezes at night.[31] If the earth were to rotate too rapidly, catastrophic winds would occur. However, the world now rotates at a speed which perfectly balances both cold and heat.

The Earth's Crust

The earth's crust is extremely thin, much thinner than the skin of an apple in comparison. Beneath the crust is molten lava. If the earth was only ten feet thicker on the outside, the additional matter would have oxidized all the available oxygen out of the air when the world began, making life impossible.[32]

The Earth's Elliptical Orbit

The earth is moving around the sun at the perfect speed. It does not move in a circular motion, but more like a football-shaped orbit. The earth is traveling at a rate of 64,800 miles an hour. If that rate was slowed by even just one-third, life would be burned up, as the earth would be pulled too close to the sun.

The Earth's Atmosphere

Forty miles above the earth is a thin layer of ozone. If compressed, it would be less than a quarter of an inch thick. The atmosphere shields this planet from 8 deadly rays emitted from the sun and from 20 million meteors a day traveling at speeds up to 30 miles a second.[33]

The Moon

The moon orbits the earth at a perfect distance of about 240,000 miles which creates the necessary tides upon the oceans. These tides clean up the oceans and their shores, but if the moon were to move in just one-fifth of this distance, the continents would be plunged underwater twice a day.[34]

It is difficult to examine our amazing universe

and not conclude that there was a Designer. Psalm 19:1 says, "The heavens declare the glory of God; and the firmament shows his handiwork." Romans 1:20 says, "For since the creation of the world his invisible attributes are clearly seen, being understood by the things that are made, even his eternal power and Godhead, so that they are without excuse."

Although there are only four thousand stars that can be seen without a telescope, the Bible has declared that the number of the stars are as the sand on the seashore (Gen. 22:17). Modern giant telescopes have verified that there are about 10^{25} (10 million billion billion) known stars in the universe.[35] It is no small wonder 90 percent of all astronomers believe in God![36]

EVIDENCE FROM COSMOLOGY

Cosmology is the study of ideas dealing with the origin of the cosmos. One of the strongest arguments for the existence of God is the universe itself. This is referred to as the cosmological argument. The cosmological argument comes from the term "cosmos" which means universe. This is where we derive the word cosmetic. The universe is orderly and beautiful. Cosmology studies how this orderly universe came into being. Scientists know there are only three possibilities:

1. The universe created itself.
2. The universe has always existed.
3. The universe was created by an outside force that is eternal.

Let us examine all three.

OPTION 1: *The Universe Has Always Existed*

In the past, scientists believed that the universe had no beginning and that matter is eternal. This is now questioned in light of the laws of thermodynamics. Entropy takes place across the universe. The amount of hydrogen in the universe is being converted into helium in the cores of stars through the process of nuclear fusion. This process is irreversible. No new hydrogen is being formed in the universe. Hence, if the universe was infinitely old, there would be no stars and very little hydrogen remaining in our universe. Knowing that the universe had a point of origin makes option one untenable.

OPTION 2: *The Universe Created Itself*

The notion that the universe came from nothing is illogical. Nothing always produces nothing. "Nothing" by definition is something that does not exist. Hence, if something exists, then something has always existed. In other words, if there was a time when nothing existed, nothing could now exist. Logically, if something exists, then something is self-existent. Thus, either the cosmos is eternal and can account for its own origin, or the universe owes its existence to something beyond the known universe that is eternal. All evidence points to the fact that the universe is not eternal and cannot account for its own existence. Scientists who have explained origins in terms of a cosmic egg which exploded have not told us where the egg came from. If there were a cosmic egg, there must have been a cosmic bird to produce the egg. Thus, there must be something beyond the physical universe of space and time which created the cosmos.

OPTION 3: The Universe Was Created by an Eternal Being

The universe could not have a beginning and be self-existent. Self-existent entities cannot have a beginning or they are not self-existent. The universe is an effect of a cause that is beyond itself. Knowing the universe is non-eternal, it can be deduced that something first caused the universe to exist. The only logical alternative to having a First Cause is to have no cause. Thus, there must be a non-contingent being who is the Creator himself, not being created. The following outline is a summary by Norman Geisler of the cosmological argument.

1. Some things undeniably exist.

2. My non-existence is possible.

3. Whatever has the possibility not to exist is currently caused to exist by another.

4. There cannot be an infinite regress of current causes of existence.

5. Therefore, a first uncaused cause of my current existence exists.

6. This uncaused cause must be infinite,

unchanging, all-powerful, all-knowing, and all perfect.

7. This infinite being is appropriately called "God."

8. Therefore, God exists.

9. This God who exists is identical to the God described in the Christian Scriptures.

10. Therefore, the God described in the Bible exists.[37]

The evidence is overwhelming — there must be a God. That is why Paul said that any person, just by looking at the universe, knows by common sense that God exists and thus has no excuse otherwise (Rom. 1:20).

EVIDENCE FROM REVELATION

Perhaps the greatest reason we know that God exists rests in the knowledge that He has told us so. He has told us who He is, what He is like, and what His plan is for our world. The Bible reveals these truths. The Bible is no mere book of man; it is the Word of God. (This topic will be discussed in the next chapter.)

The Bible teaches that God invaded history in the person of Jesus Christ. If you wanted to tell a colony of ants of your love for them, the best way would be to become an ant. This way your message could best be understood. God did exactly this. He became a man and visited planet Earth. Thus, if one wishes to know who God is, one needs only to read the Bible. The prophecies, birth, life, miracles, death, and resurrection of Jesus Christ are powerful evidences that God lives and changes people's lives.

To really know for certain God does not exist, one would need a complete knowledge of the universe. One would have to be omniscient (all-knowing) and omnipresent (everywhere at once). Atheists challenge Christians to produce God as though he could be pulled out of a magician's hat, but the evidence of God's existence is not of that nature, but is an historical and demonstrable kind of evidence.

Denying God's existence based on the lack of a personal eyewitness experience would be similar to denying that Abraham Lincoln existed. Because we cannot see or talk to him today does not mean that he did not exist. If one examines evidence and testimony, it is verifiable that Abraham Lincoln was not a fictitious character but a person of history. Many atheists, unable to prove that God does not exist, often put the Christian on the defensive by challenging the Christian to produce evidence of God's existence. However, this evidence does exist! Much of this evidence will be explored in the following chapters of this book.

If man is really the product of a great accident, his destiny is annihilation. Our lives will have meant nothing. Our lives would be, as Shakespeare said, "full of sound and fury, signifying nothing." This is the view of the nihilist who says that life is meaningless. This view leaves man with no hope, only despair. Karl Marx, Friedrich Nietzche, Sigmund Freud, and Ernest Hemingway all died bitter and lonely men. Hemingway took his own life with a shotgun thinking that the only aspects of our lives we can control are the time and means of death.

The person who does not believe in God is often one of the saddest and loneliest individuals on earth. The future ushers in the loss of all persons and possessions he treasures. After death, this person will never see his loved ones again. He may put up a courageous front, but despair and gloom rage in the back of his mind. This person finds amazement in the wondrous universe around him but considers the universe a result of chance.

Unable to know his origin or reason for existence, this person is humiliated by an utter helplessness and brevity of life. This person carries around the ticking time bomb of death which one day will explode bringing this life to an end. Comfort is not found in knowing others will share this fate because all is lost. Life appears to him but a cruel joke. This person, only able to have enjoyed existence for a short time, finds the rug of life jerked out from under him. In reality, atheism is a philosophy void of hope.

Many atheists are more comfortable with the term agnostic. The term agnostic means "no knowledge." The Latin rendering is "ignoramus." It has become fashionable for many to deny God's existence on the grounds of being an agnostic; however, very few people in this world have done an honest investigation to find out if God exists. If God exists, then it is not wise to hold to non-decision agnosticism. The stakes are eternal life. A person who remains an agnostic until death gains nothing and loses everything.

Suppose a doctor told you that you had a terminal illness which would take your life, but you had a chance to recover if you had surgery. To indefinitely postpone your decision would surely mean death. Most would take their chances with the surgery, hoping for some type of cure.

Agnosticism is not an intellectual philosophy which gives a basis for not believing in God. Agnosticism is actually a form of "suppressing" the truth by which man avoids evidences which point to the existence of God. Hence, Paul wrote, "For the wrath of God is revealed from heaven against all ungodliness and unrighteousness of men, who *suppress* the truth in unrighteousness because what may be known of God is manifest in them, for God has shown it to them" (Rom. 1:18-19). The evidence for God's existence is not only external but internal. Ecclesiastes 3:11 says that God has set eternity in the hearts of men. There is a spiritual vacuum in every person that only God can fill. This is what Augustine meant when he said, "Our hearts are restless until they find rest in thee."

Seekers who want 100 percent proof that God exists will be disappointed. The key to belief is not absolute certainty, but enough truth to put the matter beyond "a reasonable doubt." Judges in a court of law instruct juries to decide on the basis of probability, not on the need of absolute certainty.

A person who crosses a bridge can never be 100 percent certain he will make it safely to the other side. The bridge could collapse, he could trip and fall off, etc. But the lack of 100 percent assurance will not keep him from going across. He may move across with 95 percent certainty and 5 percent faith, but he still must go 100 percent across to the other side.

Perhaps you are seeking to know if God exists. Be extremely careful of demanding so much evidence that you become immune to the evidence that lies before you. No amount of evidence can ever force you to believe. For example, Jesus spoke of the agnostics of His day commenting, "If they do not hear Moses and the prophets, neither will they be persuaded though one rise from the dead" (Luke 16:31).

Christianity is not a leap into the darkness; it is a step into the light. Many non-believers think that faith is belief in an invisible nothing. Christians do not "create" God by faith. Christians have faith because of solid, historical evidence which lends itself to the truth. The Bible in Hebrews 11:1 defines "faith" as being based on "substance" and "evidence."

Based on the evidence that you have just read, are you ready to become a Christian? If you are, you must understand that becoming a Christian is more than just believing in God (James 2:19). Our problem is not intellectual; it is moral. We are in rebellion against God. This is what the Bible calls sin. The Bible requires us to repent of our sin (Luke 13:3) and commit our lives to Jesus Christ as our Lord and Saviour. The Bible says trusting Jesus is the only way a person can go to heaven (John 14:6). Being a decent person with a belief in God is not enough. We must invite Christ into our hearts by faith.

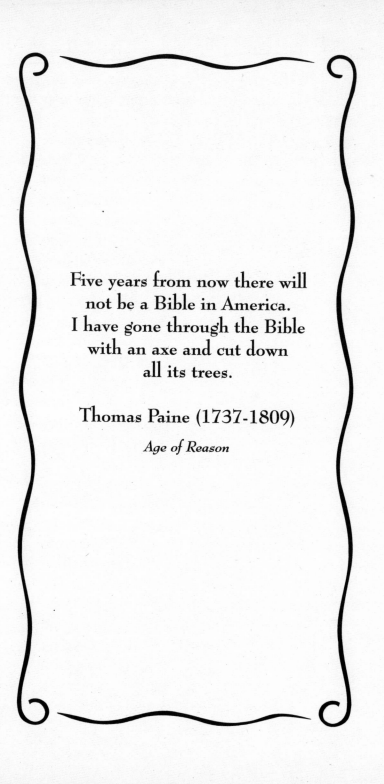

Five years from now there will
not be a Bible in America.
I have gone through the Bible
with an axe and cut down
all its trees.

Thomas Paine (1737-1809)

Age of Reason

2

THE BIBLE
IS TRUE

The Bible is the revelation of God to man. It is the record of God's dealings with man which serves as a divine compass to navigate men to eternal life. We know about God by reading about him in the Scriptures. The Bible never tries to prove the existence of God. It starts with the basic premise that God is real. The Bible purports itself to be the divine message of that God, and if the Bible were not true, it would be almost certain that its God could not be real.

There are many religions of the world, each of which claims that its god is "real." Many religions also have scriptures which claim to have the same authority as the Bible. Other scriptures include the Book of Mormon of the Church of Latter Day Saints; the Koran of Islam; the Eddas of the Scandinavians; the Tripitokas of the Buddhists; the Zendavesta of the Persians; the Analects of Confucianism; the Kojiki and Nihongi of Shintoism; and the Divine Principle of the Unification Church (the Moonies). The Bible emphatically proclaims that all other gods are false and that there is only one true God (Ps. 96:4-5).

So how can we be so sure the Bible is written by the true God? After all, was not the Bible just written by a group of men? How can one know for sure that the Bible is true and can be trusted? Many say, "What does it matter if I believe the Bible; I believe in God, isn't that enough?" If you believe in God and you don't believe in the Bible, is your god really the God of the Bible? Of course not! If your god is not the God of the Bible, how do you know that your god could be real? You do not.

It is illogical to deny the teachings of the Bible and yet affirm belief in the God of the Bible. Worshiping a god other than the God of the Bible is the worship of a false god. The Bible warns against worshiping false gods (Exod. 20:3). The Bible teaches that there is only one God and that the only true God is the God of the Bible.

Since the beginning of humankind, people have not liked to obey the Word of God. Throughout history people have rejected the true God and sought to create their own god, and because of this our world is filled with false religions and false gods. New cults are being spawned frequently as people turn away from the God of the Bible.

The question of believing in the Bible is a crucible test of determining which God you believe in. Belief in the Bible is no small matter. The stakes are eternal. Thus, for someone to declare that the Bible is not true is of grave consequence. Many attempts have been made to prove that the Bible is false, but these attempts have miserably failed. The evidence that the Bible is true is overwhelming.

In the following list, ten major evidences are offered as to why the Bible is true. This list, by no means exhaustive, contains more than enough evidence to demonstrate the uniqueness of the Bible.

EVIDENCE FROM PROPHECIES

The Old Testament contains well over 2,000 predictive prophecies, which are very specific and detailed. One of the main reasons the Bible contains so many prophecies is so that in their fulfillment, the divine origin of the Scriptures may be established. Isaiah 46:9-11 records: "Remember the former things of old, for I am God, and there is no other; I am God, and there is none like me, declaring the end from the beginning, and from ancient times things that are not yet done."

Human wisdom is unable to predict the future; this is something which can only be accomplished by the omniscience of God. Prophecy is not mere guessing or conjecture; rather, prophecy is the prediction of future events with absolute accuracy. To be wrong in any way or detail nullifies the value of the prophecy.

The standard for prophecy in the Bible is 100

percent accuracy. Deuteronomy 18:21-22 gives us the test of a prophet: "And if you say in your heart, 'how shall we know the word which the Lord has not spoken?' — When a prophet speaks in the name of the Lord, if the thing does not happen or come to pass, that is the thing which Lord has not spoken; the prophet has spoken it presumptuously; you shall not be afraid of him." If one could find any wrong prophecy in the Bible, one could demonstrate that the Bible is not the Word of God.

The ability to predict the future is the unanswerable argument whether or not one is from God or merely a pretender. God's challenge is recorded in Isaiah 41:21-23: "Present your case, says the Lord. Bring forth your strong reasons, says the King of Jacob. Let them bring forth and show us what will happen; let them show the former things, what they were, that we may consider them, and know the latter end of them; or declare us things to come. Show the things that are to come hereafter, that we may know that you are gods."

Only in the Bible does one find predictive prophecy. This important verification is noticeably absent from all other major religions such as Islam, Buddhism, Zoroastrianism, or in the writings of Confucius and Lao-tse. Other self-proclaimed prophets such as Nostradamus, Mother Shipton, Edgar Cayce, and Jean Dixon have delivered prophecies of which almost all have failed. The few which could be deemed as true are for the most part nebulous, general, and capable of multiple meanings. No being outside of an omniscient God can predict the future. Finite man peers across a chasm of darkness through which he cannot even predict what a day may bring forth. Yet, God has predicted legions of events which would occur in the future, thus proving he is all-knowing, all-mighty God. Such prophetic ability demonstrated in the Bible leaves us with no alternative but to believe that God himself is its author. Isaiah 45:21 declares, "Who has declared this from ancient time? Who has told it from that time? Have not I, the Lord? And there is no other God besides me; a just God and a Savior; there is none beside me."

Religions such as Jehovah's Witnesses and Mormonism are laden with many false prophecies and errors which create serious doubt as to their credibility. But the Bible has never failed in any single aspect of predictive prophecy.

The Bible records many instances of specific, detailed prophecies which were given hundreds of years in advance of the fulfillment. One example is Isaiah predicting that a man named Cyrus would rebuild the temple (which was still standing in his day!) in Jerusalem (Isa. 44:28). Cyrus, the Persian king, was born 150 years later. He released the Jews from their 70 years captivity in order that they might return to their homeland for the rebuilding of Jerusalem and the temple.

The Bible also predicted the fall of great cities and civilizations. All such prophecies have occurred. The following chart lists just a few examples of such prophecies.

In many of these prophecies, the exact details of the destruction were predicted. More than 100 specific prophecies exist detailing the destruction of

SELECTED PROPHECIES

Civilization	Prophecy Location	Judgment	Fulfillment
Tyre	Ezekiel 26:7-21	Destruction, never rebuilt	By Nebuchadnezzar (in 585-573 B.C.) and Alexander the Great (in 332 B.C.)
Sidon	Ezekiel 28:22-23	Blood flow in streets; destruction but no extinction	By Persians in 351 B.C.
Thebes, Egypt	Ezekiel 30:14-16	Broken up and	Lies in ruins destroyed
Edom	Ezekiel 35:3-4 Isaiah 18	Perpetual desolation,	Disappeared after the Fall of Jerusalem in A.D. 70
Gaza, Philistia	Zephaniah 2:4	Abandoned, baldness	Totally disappeared, buried under sand dunes
Bethel	Jeremiah 47:5 Amos 3:14-15	Brought to nothing	The original Bethel disappeared
Babylon	Isaiah 13:19-22	Destroyed, uninhabitable	Final destruction in A.D. 4
Nineveh	Nahum 1-3 Zephaniah 2:13	Destroyed and desolated	Disappeared in 6th century B.C.
Samaria	Micah 1-6	Destroyed, foundation uncovered, would become vineyard	By Sargon, 722 B.C.; Alexander, 331 B.C.; and John Hyrcanus, 120 B.C.
Capernaum	Matt. 11:20-23	Go down to Hades	Disappeared after A.D. 800

Babylon. Babylon was the greatest city of the ancient world. The historian Herodotus records that its walls were 200 feet tall and 87 feet thick. Three hundred-foot towers extended above the walls which enclosed an area of 196 square miles. The Bible not only predicted its destruction, but prognosticated that because of the wrath of God, it would become desolate and uninhabitable (Jer. 50:13). Today Babylon lies in a heap of ruins in the middle of the desert.

In addition to the many prophecies of the Gentile nations, the Bible has much to say about the Jewish people. Deuteronomy 28 foretells how they would be removed from their land if they were disobedient to God. God predicted that because of their disobedience, they would be scattered across the earth in unfamiliar lands (Lev. 26). The nation of Israel did indeed fall into idolatry and was removed from her homeland and later returned. They were removed a second time in A.D. 70 when the Romans destroyed Jerusalem as predicted by Jesus Christ (Luke 19:43,4; Matt. 24:2).

It was prophesied that the Jews would be scattered but would preserve their identity. For 1,900 years Jews wandered the earth being scattered and persecuted, yet Jesus predicted that the Jewish race would be intact when He comes again. So why does one never hear of Hittites, Philistines, Hivites, Moabites, Jebusites, or Ammonites? Consider the truth of the Scriptures: the Jewish people are still here today.

The Bible also predicted that though they would be scattered, they would one day return to their homeland (Ezek. 36; Amos 9). For years people said this would be impossible, yet in 1948 the Jews returned to their homeland from all parts of the earth.

Many other specific prophecies are recorded

concerning historic events and the coming of the Messiah. These will be discussed later in reference to their fulfillment in Jesus Christ. Space does not permit the listing of prophecy after prophecy which have been meticulously predicted and fulfilled. All of this points to the fact that the Bible is true. God has given us overwhelming evidence that the Bible is true so that we will heed its message. Logically, if what God said about the destruction of heathen nations because of wickedness and unbelief is true, it holds that the Bible is also truthful in what it teaches about sin, eternal life, and salvation. Just as God judged people in the past for rejecting Him, He will judge men for rejecting Him in the future.

In order that you might know the Bible is true, God has validated His word through predictive prophecy. In a world of many beliefs and many religious books, you can know that the Bible is of divine origination.

No other religious book in the world can authenticate itself like the Bible. The Bible is true because of its superhuman prophecies.

THE EVIDENCE OF INSPIRATION

The Bible guarantees its own truthfulness by deriving its origination from the inspiration of God. The term inspiration comes from 2 Timothy 3:16 which says that "All Scripture is given by inspiration of God." The word translated as inspiration means "God-breathed" as translated by the New International Version. The Greek word for inspiration is *theopneustos* which comes from the words "God" and "breath."

Consequently, the biblical writers were not inspired in the same way a great composer writes a song. Biblical writers were instructed by God to communicate that which they had received from God (2 Pet. 1:21). God chose to deliver His divine message through men. In doing so, God did not merely dictate His message, word for word, but used the personality and style of individuals to communicate His message. God did not use men as tape recorders making the Scriptures some kind of mechanical dictation. God did not place each writer in an unconscious trance, but used the personality of each writer to deliver His message. This may be readily observed in a careful reading of Luke's Book of Acts. Because Luke was a physician, he used medical terms which gave further insights into his message.

God's use of the personalities of people in no way diminishes the Bible as the Word of God. God guided the writers to write exactly what He wanted to be written. They did not leave out anything that God wanted to be recorded. In fact, Jesus said that every word is important (Matt. 4:4). To read the words of Scripture is not to read the words of men but the words of God. This is clearly taught by the Scriptures themselves. The prophets were conscious of this as they repeatedly uttered the phrase "thus says the Lord" and "the word of the Lord came to me." Writers of the New Testament believed the entire Old Testament to be the very Word of God (Rom. 3:2). The New Testament writers often quoted an Old Testament author such as Moses using phrases such as "God said" (Gen. 2:24).

The New Testament writers recognized the authority of their message. Paul writes in 1 Corinthians 14:37, "If any man think himself to be a prophet or spiritual, let him acknowledge that the things which I write to you are the commandments of the Lord." Peter, in writing about the writings of Paul, puts them in the category of being the Scriptures (2 Pet. 3:15-16).

The doctrine of inspiration is given by divine revelation. The material in the Bible comes directly from God. Moses was not present at the creation and had to be provided with the details of the creation in a supernatural way. In other cases, men were moved to record what they had witnessed, but both methods of revelation are inspired by God.

Some people teach that only some of the Bible is inspired, thus teaching that the Bible is not the Word of God but that it only contains the Word of God. This is inconsistent with 2 Timothy 3:16 which says, "*All* Scripture is given by inspiration of God." Theologians refer to the entire Bible being inspired as "plenary verbal" inspiration of the Bible. Plenary means "all" and verbal means "word." Plenary verbal inspiration asserts that every word is God-breathed, nothing is missing, and nothing is uninspired.

The Bible is far more than just the product of some very intelligent men. The Bible is God's method of communication to us. God's process of inspiration and supervision guarantees us that the message of the Scriptures is what God intended the writers to write. Therefore, when we read the Bible, we are reading the Word of God, and because we are reading the Word of God, we know that the Bible is true.

THE EVIDENCE OF INFALLIBILITY

Because the Bible is the Word of God and God cannot lie (Isa. 55:10-11; John 17:17; Titus 1:2; Heb. 4:12), the Scriptures are totally trustworthy and are free from any mixture of error. Jesus said to the Father "Your word is truth" (John 17:17). God's word is described as "the word of truth" (2 Cor. 6:7; Col. 1:5; 2 Tim. 2:15; James 1:18). Infallibility is not a theory about the Bible; it is the teaching of Scripture itself.

Some assert that only parts of the Bible are true. If this is so, how do we know that any of it is the truth? The truth is found in the fact that the Bible is never wrong. There are no verifiable errors to be found in the Bible. There are many who have claimed to have found supposed errors in the Bible.

In the late 19th century, the Institute of Paris issued 82 errors which it believed could discredit Christianity. Since that time, all 82 difficulties have been cleared away with new discoveries. What most people claim as errors in the Bible are not "errors" but "difficulties." Inconsistencies occur when people do not take time to find out all the facts. In most cases, Bible difficulties can be cleared up with an in-depth study of the problem. Two things should be understood at this point: lack of understanding is not an error nor is an unresolved difficulty an error. Many Bible difficulties have been solved as new historical and archaeological discoveries have been made. A difficulty does not constitute an error!

There are six major kinds of difficulties found among those who attack the inerrancy of the Bible.

Faith Difficulties

Many question the accuracy of the creation account of Adam and Eve, the Noachic flood, the crossing of the Red Sea during the Exodus, the story of Jonah, Christ's walking on water, or even the resurrection of Jesus. But these are actually questions of faith. Jesus confirmed the accounts of Adam and Eve, Noah, and Jonah as being historical fact (Matt. 12:40, 19:4). To reject the above stories is to reject the authority and truthfulness of Jesus. If Jesus were found to be mistaken on these issues, could He not also be mistaken on the larger issues of salvation and eternal life?

This point is illustrated in Jesus' healing of the paralytic. Jesus proved that what He said about spiritual matters was true by performing a verifiable physical healing: "Which is easier to say to the paralytic, 'Your sins are forgiven you,' or to say, 'Arise, take up your bed, and walk?' But that you may know that the Son of Man has power on earth to forgive sins." — He said to the paralytic, "I say to you arise, take up your bed, and go to your house" (Mark 2:9-11). Jesus emphasized this same truth when He said, "If I have told you earthly things, and you do not believe, how will you believe if I tell you heavenly things?" (John 3:12).

Some would try to hold that the Bible is authoritative on matters of faith but may be mistaken in other areas. The Bible does not contain two sets of verses; it is of a holistic nature, and if two kinds of verses in the Bible were found, who would decide what was what? Finite humans cannot be the final judge of difficulties. We often seek to discredit what we cannot understand. Just because we do not know "how" all the miracles in the Bible occurred does not mean they did not happen. The top scientists in the world have great difficulty understanding the writings of Albert Einstein. How much more difficult is it then for finite humans to understand the infinite God?

A certain man once came up to a Christian and said, "I have a problem believing that a man could survive for three days in the belly of a whale," to which the Christian replied, "That's not what's so difficult to believe. I have more difficulty trying to understand how God could make a man and how God could make a fish." The denial of the miraculous stories in the Bible is not a question of accuracy but of faith.

Language Difficulties

The Bible describes events phenomenologically or figuratively — which is to describe things as they appear to be. The Scriptures use figures of speech such as the sun rising and setting. Many would charge the Bible with an error at this point. Modern scientific knowledge tells us that the sun does not rise or set but that the earth rotates. However, we use the same phrases today and are not charged with error. Figures of speech are not errors as such.

Scientific Difficulties

Some hold that the Bible is an antiquated religious book filled with primitive, pre-scientific views of the universe. Thus, some would say that the Bible should only be read for spiritual truths because it errs in matters of objective science and history. Such persons would say that "the Bible is not a book of science but of religion." However the Bible never purports itself to be a scientific handbook loaded down with formulas, charts, and hypotheses. Such books of science, even in our own day, go out of date very quickly, and even the most current encyclopedias must constantly be rewritten because new knowledge is coming available at an astounding rate. Yet one searches in vain for any scientific errors in the Bible. One cannot find notions of a flat earth, spontaneous generation, or Ptolemaic astronomy. While the Bible does not try to teach chemistry or biology, it never stands in conflict with verified science in any way. In all places that the Bible deals with scientific matters, it is completely accurate.

Factual Difficulties

Many of the supposed errors in the Bible deal with statistics. For example, Matthew 28:2 mentions one angel at Christ's tomb and John 20:12 lists two, but is this a real contradiction? If there were two angels, it is certainly reasonable to say that mathematically there was one, for only one spoke. He could easily be referring to the one who spoke. Matthew never says that there was "only" one. In other places, different authors describe the same event. One may use a rounded off number, the other uses an exact number. There are numerous examples of this type of difficulty in the Bible. However, a closer study will always reveal a logical explanation. While not every single Bible discrepancy has been totally resolved, all have a satisfactory answer. To say the Bible is full of errors is a statement which has no factual basis. With new archaeological discoveries confirming the accuracy of the Scriptures, there has never been a time in history when we could be so confident in the factual truthfulness of the Bible.

Doctrinal Difficulties

These are very minor problems. An example is Paul saying that we are saved by faith alone, not of works (Eph. 2:8). Whereas James says we are justified by works (James 2:18). Paul is emphasizing that one cannot be saved by good works. James states that saving faith is expressed in the form of works. James 2:18 says, "I will show you my faith by my works." James is speaking of "verification" and Paul was speaking of faith as a " prerequisite" for salvation which is faith alone. They were saying the same thing — Paul was referring to pre-salvation, and James was speaking of post-salvation Christian service. Paul recognized the role of works after salvation in Ephesians 2:10: "For we are his workmanship, created in Christ Jesus for good works." Such doctrinal difficulties are easily resolved by examining the passages in light of the context and the author's intention.

Ethical Difficulties

An example would be putting God's commandment "You shall not murder" (Exod. 20:13) against the Old Testament authorization of capital punishment. The commandment in Exodus applies to murder, which is taking the life of an "innocent" person. The Bible forbids murder but allows capitol punishment. Capitol punishment is taking the life of a "guilty" person for the reason of justice and deterrence. To believe that the Bible contradicts itself in forbidding murder but advocating capitol punishment is a mistake of over-generalization. The murder of innocent people and taking the life of the guilty for punishment are clearly different matters. Ethical difficulties are easily resolved through careful study of the issues in their full context and meaning.

Regardless of the kind of difficulty found, not one single "irreconcilable error" is to be found in the pages of Scripture. The Bible can be trusted as truthful as seen in its own infallibility and inerrancy.

THE EVIDENCE OF TRANSMISSION

Because the Bible is an ancient book, some wonder if they are reading the original message of the Bible. The Bible is the most trustworthy document from all of antiquity. In standards of reliability, the Bible stands without any single peer.

The original autographs of the Old Testament were written on papyrus. Papyrus deteriorates at a very rapid rate. Because of this, scribes were employed to copy the books of the Old Testament. These scribes believed the Scriptures to be the Word of God and went to great lengths to eliminate error. They followed strict Jewish traditions which even dictated how many columns and lines could be on a page, counting every line, word, and letter to find any mistakes. Any copy with even one mistake was destroyed. Because of this, the Old Testament has been preserved in its original form. Prior to 1947 the oldest existing Old Testament copy was the Massoretic Text which is dated about A.D. 900. In 1947 the Dead Sea Scrolls were found at Qumran. Many of the scrolls dated back to around 150 B.C. making them almost 1,000 years older than the Massoretic Text. The Dead Sea Scrolls read identical to the Massoretic Text, both of which are identical to the Hebrew translations in our own Bibles. Only a small percent of variation can be found, all of which can be attributed to variations in spelling.

The reliability of the New Testament is also beyond reproach. More than 24,000 partial and complete copies of the New Testament are available today. No other document of antiquity can even come close to such large numbers. Homer's *Iliad* is second with a mere 643 existing manuscripts. So sparse are copies of ancient classical works that 20 copies would be a lofty number of manuscripts. In addition to the New Testament manuscripts, there are over 86,000 quotations of the New Testament from the Early Church fathers. So thorough are these quotations that all but 11 verses of the New Testament can be reconstructed from this material, which dates less than 200 years after the coming of Jesus.

Not only are the New Testament documents superior because of their great numbers, but also because of the time span existing between the original autographs and their copies. Unlike Buddha, whose sayings were not recorded until 500 years after his death, all the books of the New Testament were probably written within 30 years of the death of Jesus. The earliest copies of our existing New

Testament begin at A.D. 125. In comparison, Homer's *Iliad* has a time span exceeding over 500 years between the time of writing and the oldest manuscript. No book in antiquity can compare with the New Testament in the number of manuscripts or in the interval of time between the originals and the copies. Compare the New Testament with the top works of antiquity in the chart on the following page.

The New Testament in comparison to other ancient manuscripts is virtually free from any corruption. Textual critics have found only one-half of one percent differs. Thus, 99 $\frac{1}{2}$ percent of the New Testament has no variation. These variations for the most part deal with matters of spelling or word order. Not one single variant has any bearing on a doctrine of faith. In any case, the Church has in its possession 100 percent of the New Testament. Such confidence cannot be attributed to any other piece of classical literature. The accuracy of transmission in the manuscripts of the Bible testifies to their truthfulness.

EVIDENCE FROM ARCHAEOLOGY

Prior to the 19th century there were many facts contained within the historical narratives which were not verifiable. In other words, there were many people, places, battles, and dates which were only found in the Bible. Severe attacks on the Bible originated in the 19th century which asserted that the writers of the Scriptures resorted to folklore and myth to validate their spiritual teachings. These critics asserted that the people and places recorded in the

COMPARISON OF MAJOR WORKS OF ANTIQUITY

Author/Work	No. of Copies	When Written	Earliest Copy	Time Span
New Testament	24,000+	A.D. 40-100	A.D. 125	25 yrs.
Homer	653	900 B.C.	400 B.C.	500 yrs.
Pliny the Younger (History)	7	A.D. 61-113	A.D. 850	750 yrs.
Suetonius	8	A.D. 75-160	A.D. 950	800 yrs.
Tacitus (Minor Works)	1	A.D. 100	A.D. 1000	900 yrs.
Caesar	10	100-44 B.C.	A.D. 900	1000 yrs.
Tacitus (Annals)	20	A.D. 100	A.D. 1100	1000 yrs.
Aristophanes	10	450-385 B.C.	A.D. 900	1200 yrs.
Plato (Tetralogies)	7	427-347 B.C.	A.D. 900	1200 yrs.
Herodotus (History)	8	480-425 B.C.	A.D. 900	1300 yrs.
Demosthenes	200*	383-322 B.C.	A.D. 1100	1300 yrs.
Thucydides (History)	8	460-400 B.C.	A.D. 900	1300 yrs.
Sophocles	193	496-406 B.C.	A.D. 1000	1400 yrs.
Aristotle	49+	384-322 B.C.	A.D. 1100	1400 yrs.
Euripides	9	480-406 B.C.	A.D. 1100	1500 yrs.
Catullus	3	54 B.C.	A.D. 1550	1600 yrs.

*All from one copy   + From any one work [1]

early parts of Scriptures were mere legend.

Just as these theories of higher criticism seemed on the verge of destroying the integrity of the Scriptures, an explosion of archaeological evidence

PAST CHARGES BY CRITICS	ANSWERED BY ARCHAEOLOGY
Moses could not have written Pentateuch because he lived before the invention of writing.	Writing existed many centuries before Moses.
Abraham's home city of Ur does not exist.	Ur was discovered. One of the columns had the inscription "Abram."
The city built of solid rock called "Petra" does not exist.	Petra was discovered.
The "Hittites" did not exist.	Hundreds of references to the amazing Hittite civilization have been found. One can even get a doctorate in Hittite studies at the University of Chicago.
Belshazzar was not a real king of Babylon; he is not found in the records.	Tablets of Babylonia describe the reign of this corgent and son of Nabonidus.

silenced the critics. In the early 19th century scientists began to dig beneath the surface of the earth. They found ancient cities and civilizations they never knew existed. At a time when the Scriptures were said to be void of historical confirmation, the stones began to cry out otherwise.

In the last century numerous archaeological discoveries have been made which vindicate the historical narratives of the Old Testament. Because these narratives are quite specific, they easily lend themselves to archaeological investigation. Over 25,000 sites have been discovered which have a connection with the Old Testament period. Not only have these discoveries provided external confirmation to hundreds of scriptural assertions, but not one single archaeological discovery has ever contradicted a biblical assertion. Places and people from the Old Testament began to surface with the discoveries of ancient civilizations in Egypt, Babylonia, Assyria, and Palestine. So many of the past criticisms have been refuted that it seems that God is trying to send a message to modern scientific men. The chart on the following page lists some of the great archaeological discoveries and their significance to the Old Testament.

The New Testament was also called into question in the 19th century. The Book of Acts was thought to be a forgery from the mid-second century, but as the evidence poured in from modern archaeological discoveries, Luke was found to be an historian of the highest order. Many places such as the Pool of Bethesda, the Pool of Siloam, Jacob's Well, and Pilate's residence in Jerusalem have been clearly identified.

The Bible has been verified historically, which demonstrates that it is no forgery. In every instance, without exception, where the Bible has been examined in light of archaeological evidence, it is true in what it says.

THE EVIDENCE OF UNITY

The Bible towers above all other books as the all-time best seller in history. Over 40 authors combined to write the 66 books found in the Bible. It was written over a span of 1,500 years, in three languages, and was composed in 13 countries on three continents. The Bible was written by men from all walks of life including kings, peasants, herdsmen, tax collectors, philosophers, statesmen, fishermen, poets, and scholars. It uses various literary forms

ARCHAEOLOGICAL FIND	SIGNIFICANCE
Mari Tablets	Over 20,000 cuneiform tablets, which date back to Abraham's time period, explain many of the patriarchal traditions of Genesis.
Ebla Tablets	Over 20,000 tablets, many containing law similar to the Deuteronomy law code. The previously thought fictitious five cities of the plain in Genesis 14 (Sodom, Gomorrah, Admah, Zeboiim, and Zoar) are identified.
Nuzi Tablets	They detail customs of the 14th and 15th century parallel to the patriarchal accounts such as maids producing children for barren wives.
Black Stele	Proved that writing and written laws existed three centuries before the Mosaic laws.
Temple Walls of Karnak, Egypt	Signifies a tenth century B.C. reference to Abraham.
Laws of Eshnunna (c. 1950 B.C.) Lipit-Ishtar Code (c. 1860 B.C.) Laws of Hammurabi (c. 1700)	Show that the law codes of the Pentateuch were not too sophisticated for that period.
Ras Shamra Tablets	Provide information on Hebrew poetry.
Lachish Letters	Describe Nebuchadnezzar's invasion of Judah and give insight into the time of Jeremiah.
Gedaliah Seal	Gedaliah is spoken of in 2 Kings 25:22..
Cyrus Cylinder	Authenticates the biblical description of Cyrus' decree to allow the Jews to rebuild the temple in Jerusalem (see 2 Chron. 36:23; Ezra 1:2-4).
Moabite Stone	Gives information about Omri, the sixth king of Israel.
Black Obelisk of Shalmaneser III	Illustrates how Jehu, king of Israel, had to submit to the Assyrian king.
Taylor Prism	Contains an Assyrian text which details Sennacherib's attack on Jerusalem during the time of Hezekiah, king of Israel.

such as history, poetry, proverbs, preaching, prophecy, parables, allegories, biography, drama, exposition, law, and letters. Yet, in spite of all this diversity, the Bible contains a vast unity. This unity is so unique that the books of the Bible form a unit, such that the Bible is not a mere collection of books, it is just one Book.

Some have proposed that the Bible is just the invention of men. However such a theory of human conspiracy is ruled out by the vast time span involved. Not only would such a conspiracy require someone who could make up the fictitious story, it would require legions of actors and civilizations to act out the story in history. No human conspiracy could supervise such a 1,500-year project.

Only an omniscient, all-controlling, all-directing architect could construct such a cosmic drama. Every single author in the Bible is in perfect harmony with all the other writers in the areas of doctrine, ethics, faith, and the plan of salvation. One cannot even find a handful of books over a span of 1,500 years which all agree with one another without any conflicts whatsoever. Yet, all 66 books of the Bible are in perfect harmony.

The Bible maintains an unmistakable organic unity. The Bible centers around one central theme — redemption. The drama begins in Genesis in which the fall of man is recorded, showing man's need for redemption. The promise of a Redeemer is given. A sacrificial system was set up to represent pictorially the process of redemption. The New Testament records the fulfillment of redemption which is found in the person and work of Jesus Christ.

The logical order of the Bible is truly amazing. The Old Testament is the preparation for the coming of Christ. The theme of Christ runs throughout the entire Bible. Just as the British navy's rope has a scarlet thread through it to prevent theft, the Bible contains a crimson aura that surfaces in every book of the Bible. The entire Bible exists to reveal Jesus Christ; He is the sole reason for every event in the Bible. The word "gospel" literally means "God's story." Bible history is actually His-story.

The Library of Congress contains a unique copy of the Emancipation Proclamation. The face of Lincoln is revealed by the shading of certain letters in the text. In the Bible a beautiful picture of Christ also emerges. He appears in the Old Testament in type and prophecy. The Bible is a complete unity thought out by a divine mind. The New Testament is the perfect fulfillment of the Old Testament. The Old Testament closes in Malachi where the promise of the appearance of the Messiah is the next major event. Four hundred years passed before the New Testament writings began.

The New Testament is not a separate later addition to the Old Testament, but the New maintains an indissoluble relationship to the Old. They are theological twin pillars which support the same redemptive message. There is nothing in the New Testament which cannot be found in the Old Testament:

The New is in the Old contained;
    the Old is by the New explained;
The New is in the Old concealed;
    the Old is by the New revealed;

The New is in the Old foreshown;
the Old is in the New full-grown.[2]

The pattern of both Testaments are identical:

Themes	Old Testament	New Testament
Revelation	Pentateuch (1st 5 books)	Revelation (last book)
History	Joshua — Esther	Gospels (1st 4 books)
Devotion	Job — Song of Solomon	Book of Acts
Prophecy	Isaiah — Malachi	Epistles

    The New Testament complements the Bible in every way. Each Testament serves as a column which holds up the entire structure. The structural unity of the Bible is symmetrically arranged so that it displays perfect agreement and order.

    There was no chance of human conspiracy. The first writers had no way of knowing what others would write centuries later. The Bible towers as a great temple with 66 perfectly laid stones, and as with any structure, there must be an architect who provided the design. So complete is the unity of the Bible that no stone dare be taken away or added to its structure (see Rev. 22:19). This type of unity is a miracle of God which serves to alert mankind to the truthfulness of the Bible.

THE EVIDENCE OF AUTHENTICATION

    One of the greatest reasons for believing that the Bible is true is that Jesus believed in the truthfulness of the Scriptures. To reject Scripture is in essence to reject Jesus. It would be very unusual for someone to believe in Jesus as Saviour and Lord and yet believe that Jesus was wrong on the issue of the Scriptures. Jesus used the Old Testament to validate who He was (Luke 24:27, 44; John 5). He believed that the Scripture could not be broken (John 10:35). Jesus held that every word and letter was important (Matt. 5:17-19). He believed that doctrinal error came from misunderstanding the Scriptures and rebuked the Pharisees for making their traditions equal with the Scriptures (Matt. 15:6).

In controversies, Jesus simply quoted the Scripture to end the debate (Matt. 4:4-10; John 8:17). Jesus authoritatively answered His critics with questions like: "It is written," "Have you not read," and "Search the Scriptures." Jesus even used Scripture to overcome the temptations of Satan (Matt. 4:4).

The writings of the New Testament make it clear that Jesus did not believe the Old Testament to be a collection of legends. Jesus never questioned the integrity of any Old Testament book. He believed the writers were those whose names were on the writings.

The New Testament verified the historicity of over 40 Old Testament people, not counting the genealogical lists. It is difficult to say that one could accept the New Testament as historical but not the Old Testament. If one truly believes the New Testament, one cannot reject any of the Old Testament. Jesus believed in the accuracy of the Old Testament and believed it to be the Word of God.

It is illogical to affirm Jesus as the Son of God but assert that the Scriptures contain errors. If it were true that there were errors in the Bible, there

OLD TESTAMENT REFERENCES ACKNOWLEDGED BY JESUS	
Creation	Mark 10:6
Adam and Eve	Matt. 19:3-6
Murder of Abel	Luke 11:51
Sodom & Gomorrah	Luke 10:12
Noah	Luke 17:26-27
Exodus	John 6:49
Miracles of Elijah	Luke 4:25-27
Abraham, Jacob, & Isaac	Luke 20:37-38
Moses, author of Pentateuch	John 5:46-47
Isaiah wrote all of Isaiah	Matt. 4:14-16; 12:17; John 12:38-41
Daniel's prophecies as truth	Matt. 24:15
Jonah	Matt. 12:39-41

are only four possibilities regarding the statements of Jesus.

First, Jesus was a fraud and lied about the Scriptures. It insults the intelligence of the reader to think for one moment that Jesus was a devious, evil, sinister liar. Jesus loved humanity. The entire life of Jesus was of kindness. The character of a person goes hand in hand with the claims of a person.

Second, Jesus knew there were errors but covered them up to accommodate the beliefs of his day. This is known as "The Accommodation Theory." This theory holds that Jesus went along with erroneous views in order to present His message to listeners. This theory is not consistent with the gospels which show that Jesus never accepted the mistaken views of His time. Jesus often refuted wrong traditions saying, "You have heard that it was said. . . .

But I say to you . . ." (Matt. 5). If Jesus had taught error as being truth, He would have been guilty of deception. However, the New Testament asserts that Jesus never sinned nor said anything that would not be trustworthy (1 Pet. 2:22).

Third, there were errors in the Bible but Jesus was ignorant of them. If Jesus was mistaken, He certainly was not who He claimed to be and was a fraud. If the errors were in the Bible and Jesus was not aware of them, He could not have been the Son of God as He claimed.

Fourth, the view of Jesus was correct. The Bible is free from errors. Thus it is illogical for a believer to reject the truthfulness of Scripture. For the Christian, the authority of Christ settles the issue of the truthfulness of the Bible.

THE EVIDENCE OF INTEGRITY

The Bible contains no traces of being a forgery. If the Bible was the invention of human minds, the characters of the Bible would have been cast in a favorable light. Yet, the great victories of the Israelites are never attributed to courage or superior strategy. The weaknesses of men are exposed, as the greatness of God is extolled. Even the greatest heroes of God are exposed when they erred in their own judgment. A forged Bible would have tried to cover up all negative elements.

However, the writers of the Bible did not try to cover up the facts. One finds the prominent disciples arguing, struggling with doubts, and giving up hope. The New Testament writers were committed to telling the truth as eyewitnesses. They wrote their writings in the same generation as the actual events. If they did not tell the truth, there were plenty of people around that could refute them. Because most of the New Testament was written between A.D. 40 and 70, there was not enough time for myths about Christ to be told without being refuted.

The New Testament writers had nothing to gain by falsifying information. Even when subjected to persecution and martyrdom, they maintained that what they had preached and taught was truth. No atheist would be willing to die for such an elaborate religious sham. Why would the disciples risk eternal damnation over a religious enterprise from which they would not receive material or financial benefits? Only men of great spiritual integrity would have maintained their position of the Scriptures under such intense life-threatening pressures.

THE EVIDENCE OF CANONICITY

The question which invariably arises when speaking of the Scriptures is, "How does one know which books in today's Bible are the right ones?" It is important to note at this point that a group of men did not just arbitrarily select a group of books to be used in compiling the Bible. They only officially "recognized" which books had always been upheld as being scriptural.

The processes of formation for the Old Testament and New Testament differed. The Old Testament developed over a period of 1,100 years. When Moses produced the Torah, it was immediately identified as inspired and authoritative. In time, other works were added which were deemed to be authenticated by God. A threefold division arose of Law, Prophets, and Writings. These writings eventually became a completed collection and came to be referred to as "the Scripture(s)." The Christian Church accepted these completed works in their entirety as found in the Hebrew Bible (Matt. 22:29; John 10:35, 19:36; Acts 18:24; Rom. 1:2; 2 Pet. 1:20).

The New Testament developed in a much shorter time span. Because Jesus was the promised Messiah of the Old Testament, His words were considered as divine and authoritative. The early Christians produced works which recorded the words of Jesus called "the gospels." The letters of the apostles and Paul were reproduced and circulated along with gospels throughout all the churches (Col. 4:16; 2 Pet. 3:16). These writings begin with the Book of James (c. A.D. 45) and conclude with the Revelation. The collection of these works became known as the "Canon." The word *canon* is a Greek term which meant a "list" or "index." The process of canonization was not a formal process by which Church leaders all met to decide which books could be included in the canon. Books which were deemed to be inspired by God were immediately treated as authoritative. These works began to be assimilated into a collection of sacred writings.

A crisis in the fourth century caused the Church to give a formal statement on which books were canonical. In A.D. 397, a Church Council was held in Carthage which endorsed the exact 27 books of the New Testament we now regard as canonical. These 27 books were all apostolic in origin, authoritative in spiritual content, and accepted universally among the orthodox churches. These tests were used at the council to eliminate the spurious gospels and epistles written by heretical groups. This process of canonization has ensured that today's Bible contains only the books which were attested as being inspired by God.

THE EVIDENCE OF PRESERVATION

The Bible has been the most persecuted book in all of history. For 2,000 years every possible effort has been made to undermine the authority of the Bible. Attacked by emperors, popes, kings, and scholars, the Bible has endured attacks by intellectual, political, philosophical, scientific, and physical forces.

The earliest attacks came in the form of arguments from Celsus, Prophyry, and Lucien. It was next attacked by the emperors who made it a capital offense to have a Bible. The fiercest opposition came in A.D. 303 from the Roman emperor Diocletion. Every family caught with a Bible was put to death. Every confiscated Bible was burned, and thousands of Christians were slain. So successful was Diocletion's attack that he thought he had brought an end to the Bible. He erected a column and inscribed the words *Extincto nomine Christianorum*, which means "The name of the Christians has been extinguished." His efforts failed. Within just ten years Christianity became the official religion of the Roman Empire.

Great thinkers throughout the centuries have sought to destroy the Bible. The famous French philosopher of the 18th century, Voltaire, attacked the Bible and predicted that within 50 years it would be forgotten. However, 50 years after his death, the Geneva Bible Society used Voltaire's printing press and home to produce Bibles.

Similarly, two centuries ago Thomas Paine attacked Christianity in his book entitled *The Age of Reason*. Paine believed his arguments were powerful enough to dispose of the Bible permanently. He asserted that within a few years the Bible would be out of print. Two hundred years later Paine and his book have been relegated to antiquity, yet the Bible remains the all-time best seller since its first printed copy.

How would one regard a man who had been hanged, poisoned, drowned, burned, and yet would not die? One would regard this person as superhuman. This is how the Bible should be viewed. It has been burned, persecuted, mocked, and torn to pieces, yet never damaged. The Bible is a superhuman book. If it were the work of men, it would have long since been destroyed.

If the Bible were merely a human book, its survival would be difficult to account for. Books, like humans, have a very short life span. The average book only survives about 20 years. The Bible, with its thousands of ancient manuscripts, towers above any other work which has survived a thousand years. But one need not go back to the ancient past to make comparisons. Today, more has been written about the Bible than any other 1,000 books put together. It has now been translated into over 1,700 languages.

How remarkable for a book which for centuries was pitted against the most intelligent and powerful forces in the world. During such dark times, only a persecuted and despised minority sought to uphold the Bible. No powerful army ever defended the Bible, but for every Bible destroyed, thousands have appeared. Like the three Hebrew men thrown into the fiery furnace, the Bible could not be burned out of existence. Out of the ashes arose the reproductive seeds of multiplication. Like a mythical Hydra with nine heads, each time one head was cut asunder, two more appeared. Every persecution brought against the Bible has resulted in the multiplication of the Scriptures. Throughout history, many times it seemed as though the Bible had been driven out of existence. Though the death bell rang, the corpse would not stay buried. The hammers of the Bible's critics have long since been worn out on the anvil of the Word of God.

God himself promises the perseverance of His Word: "Heaven and earth will pass away, but My words will by no means pass away" (Matt. 24:35). Isaiah wrote over 2,500 years ago, "The grass withers, the flower fades, but the word of our God stands forever" (Isa. 40:8).

The Bible is at the same time the most loved and most hated book of all time. Why has the Bible generated so much animosity? Precisely for the simple reason that the Bible reveals the guilt of men and holds them accountable for their sins. The problems most people have with the Bible are not its alleged difficulties, but with its teachings on how sinful man is reconciled to a Holy God. Mark Twain spoke of this problem when he commented, "Most people are bothered by those passages in Scripture which they cannot understand. The Scripture which troubles me the most is the Scripture I do understand."

Dr. R. A. Torrey was once confronted by a young man who attacked the Bible. Insightfully, Torrey asked the question, "Is your life right?" The young man abandoned the conversation and quickly excused himself. Like this young man, most people have not rejected Christianity on intellectual grounds but on spiritual grounds. What about you? Have you ever honestly done an in-depth study on the veracity of the Scriptures? To reject the Bible without conclusively demonstrating it to be false is a most unwise decision. The evidence clearly favors the truthfulness of the Bible.

A man who was merely a man and said the sort of things Jesus said wouldn't be a great moral teacher. He'd either be a lunatic — on a level with a man who says he's a poached egg — or else he'd be the devil of hell. You must make your choice. Either this man was, and is, the Son of God: or else a madman or something worse. But don't let us come with any patronizing nonsense about his being a great human teacher. He hasn't left that open to us. He didn't intend to.

C.S. Lewis

Mere Christianity

3

JESUS IS GOD

J esus of Nazareth was not just another face on an already populated religious scene. Jesus made a claim, which was never made by any of the founders of the world's major religions. He claimed to be God — a claim which Buddha, Confucius, nor Mohammed never made. Such a claim cannot be ignored, it must be believed or refuted. To ignore the question of Jesus' deity is to reject Jesus himself. If Jesus is truly divine, then His coming to earth is the most important event in history. If Jesus is God, then His message of redemption is the most important message we will ever hear. Jesus not only claimed to be God, but also He claimed that His way of salvation is the only way sinful men can be restored to a right relationship with the Holy God. There is compelling evidence which demonstrates that Jesus is God and that His message is true.

THE EVIDENCE OF HISTORICITY

The message of Christianity centers around the truth that God became a man. Many present-day skeptics have asserted that Christianity is a myth invented by a group of religious extremists. Some have sought to dismiss Christianity into the realm of fiction maintaining that Christianity holds to no historical basis. Some skeptics have even questioned whether Jesus actually ever existed. Such claims are never made by knowledgeable historians. Those who have actually studied the historical authenticity of Jesus admit to being overwhelmed by the abundance of evidence that exists. Those who attempt to dismiss Christ as a myth simply do not do so on the basis of historical evidence. In fact, the evidence is so great that even if we did not have a Bible, we would still know the story of Christianity and of its Christ. The non-Christian sources in the following chart each give credence to the life of Christ.

Many other secular writers refer to Christ and Christianity; these include Epictetus, Aristides, Galenus, Lampridius, Dio Cassius, Hinnerius, Libanius, Ammianus, Marcellinus, Eunapius, Zosimus. Numerous references from Jewish rabbis also discuss the life of Jesus. Not even one of these early references ever questions whether or not Jesus actually existed, nor do any present-day historians deny the historicity of Jesus Christ.

EARLY NON-CHRISTIAN REFERENCES TO JESUS

WRITER	DATE	WRITING	RELEVANCE
Thallus	A.D. 52	Chronicle	Solar eclipse at the crucifixion
Josephus	A.D. 93	Antiquities	References John the Baptist, James, and Jesus
Pliny the Younger	A.D. 112	Letter to Trajon	Information about early Christianity
Cornelius Tacitus	A.D. 116	Annals	Information on the origin and spread of Christianity
Serenius	A.D. 117-38	Letter to Hadrian	Discusses charges brought against Christians
Suetonius	A.D. 120	Life of Nero	Reports punishment inflicted on Christians
Phlegon	A.D. 140	Olympiads	Solar eclipse at the crucifixion
Lucian of Somosata	A.D. 170	The Death of Peregrine	Hostile testimony about early Christians

THE EVIDENCE OF HISTORICAL IMPACT

Amazing similarities exist between the lives of Socrates and Jesus. Both strived to improve mankind, gathered disciples, and unjustly died; however, Socrates left his world unchanged, and his teachings became forgotten. But when Jesus departed, He had forever changed the world. The disciples of Jesus continue to carry His message around the world to this day. Why? Whereas Socrates was found to be a man, Jesus was found to be God. History has never been the same since the coming of

Jesus. History itself is divided by two epochs — before Christ (B.C.) and after Christ (A.D.). Everything is dated with reference to the birth of Jesus Christ.

Jesus never wrote a book and yet He remains the subject of more books than anyone in history. His biography, the New Testament, is the greatest selling book of all time. It gives very few details of His life but focuses on His brief three-year itinerant ministry. From this short period sprang the largest religious following in history. Few persons have ever evoked such devotion as Jesus of Nazareth. His recorded deeds and teaching have been judged as true by countless millions. Jesus is no mere mortal with an extremely high IQ, but His impact is best understood in light of His claim that He is God.

THE EVIDENCE OF MESSIANIC PROPHECIES

The Old Testament is filled with promises of the coming of the Messiah. The "Messiah" refers to the promised deliverer who would come to establish the kingdom of God. "Christ" is the Greek equivalent of the term "Messiah." Jesus is one of over 40 Jewish men who have claimed to be the Christ, so how do we know that Jesus of Nazareth is really the promised Messiah?

The Old Testament contains hundreds of specific messianic prophecies about the Messiah. Because of the volume and specific nature of the prophecies, accidental fulfillment of these prophecies is impossible according to the laws of probability. Jesus of Nazareth is the only person in history who has fulfilled every one of these prophecies.

These prophecies, found in the Old Testament, written over 400 years in advance of Jesus' birth, serve as a screening process for anyone who would claim to be the Messiah. The Old Testament meticulously recorded specific details about the Messiah so that He could be identified upon His arrival.

The fact that Jesus could fulfill all of the messianic prophecies reveals the intervention of a supernatural authority. Some would object: "What if Jesus manipulated His life to try to become the Messiah?" This is impossible in light of the fact that Jesus' enemies fulfilled many of the prophecies through their own actions. The accounts of Jesus' suffering, not to mention His resurrection from the dead, could never have been faked. The argument for Jesus being the Messiah was not recently proposed by Christians. Even before the birth of Jesus, the Jews had carefully constructed Old Testament prophecy lists concerning the Messiah. Such lists were found among the discoveries at Qumran.

Jesus based His entire ministry on the fact that He is the promised Messiah. The first disciples of Jesus followed Him because they believed He was the Christ. Jesus taught His disciples that the prophecies about Him must be fulfilled and that the entire Old Testament spoke of Him. Paul taught that Jesus Christ is the key to understanding the Old Testament (2 Cor. 3: 14-17). Ultimately, it was because Jesus claimed to be the Christ that He was put to death.

The truth of Christianity stands upon the fact that Jesus is the Christ. If it is shown that Jesus did not fulfill the messianic prophecies, then Christianity would not be true. No other religion has such a

OLD TESTAMENT PROPHECIES FULFILLED IN JESUS

PROPHECY	O.T. SCRIPTURE	N.T. FULFILLMENT
Virgin conception	Isa. 7:14	Matt. 1:22-23
Born in Bethlehem	Mic. 5:2	Luke 2:4-11
Descendant of Abraham	Gen. 12:1-3	Matt. 1:1
Descendant of Isaac	Gen. 21-12	Heb. 11:18
Tribe of Judah	Gen. 49:10	Luke 3:23
Davidic lineage	Ps. 132:11	Matt. 1:1
Miracles	Isa. 35:5-6	Matt. 9:35
Temple cleansing	Mal. 3:1	Matt. 21:12
Jewish rejection	Ps. 118:22	1 Pet. 2:7
Ascension	Ps. 68:18	Acts 1:9
Sit at right hand of God	Ps. 110:1	Heb. 1:3
Betrayed for 30 pieces of silver	Zech. 11:12-13	Matt. 27:9-10
Heralded by a messenger of the Lord	Mal. 3:1	Matt. 3:1-2
Crucified with thieves	Isa. 53:12	Luke 23:33
Side would be pierced	Zech. 12:10	John 19:34
Buried in rich man's tomb	Isa. 53:9	Matt. 27:57-60
Lots cast for his garments	Ps. 22:18	John 19:23-24
Hands and feet pierced	Ps. 22:16	Luke 23:33
Silent before accusers	Isa. 53:7	Matt. 27:12-19
Prayed for persecutors	Isa. 53:12	Matt. 23:34
Betrayed by a disciples	Ps. 41:9	Matt. 26:14-15
Betrayal money returned	Zech. 11:13	Matt. 27:3-10
Accused by false witnesses	Ps. 35:11	Matt. 26:59
Stripped	Isa. 53:5	Matt. 27:28-29
Number with criminals	sa. 53:12	Mark 15:27
Gall and vinegar offered	Ps. 69:21	Matt. 27-34
No bones broken	Ps. 34:20	John 19:33-36
Darkness during day to signal crucifixion	Amos 8:9	Matt. 27:45
Taught by parables	Ps. 78:2	Matt. 13:34-35
Betrayal money used to buy potter's field	Zech. 11:13	Matt. 27:7
Scourged and spit upon	Ps. 35:15; Isa. 50:6	Mark 14:65
Visage greatly marred	Isa. 52:14; 53:3	John 19:1-5
Suffered to bear our sins	Isa. 53:4-6; Dan. 9:26	1 Pet. 3:18
Flesh would not see corruption	Ps. 16:8-10	Acts 2:31
Resurrection	Ps. 16:8-10; 30:3	Luke 24:6, 31-34

stringent test imposed upon its leader. In Jesus Christ, 456 identifiable prophecies were uniquely fulfilled. The chances of any man fulfilling just 48 of such prophecies is a probability of 10^{157}. This figure, calculated by Peter Stoner, Professor Emeritus of Science at Westmont college, has been confirmed by the committee of the American Scientific Affiliation.[1] The fulfillment of messianic prophecies at such a high level of probability indicates a supernatural agent. The fact that Jesus is the Messiah is not just a clever guess, nor could Jesus have been an imposter who carefully arranged the fulfillment of all the messianic prophecies. To reject Jesus as Messiah requires an unbelief which runs counter to the laws of probability.

THE EVIDENCE OF MIRACLES

It is one thing to claim to be God, but it is another matter to prove it. A claim of deity must be accompanied by extraordinary evidence. One of the ways that Jesus demonstrated He was divine was by performing miracles. Miracles occur in the Bible as a means of authenticating divine revelation. When Jesus began His ministry, He unleashed a series of miracles which arrested the world's attention. Jesus healed the sick, gave sight to the blind, fed thousands of people from a handful of food, demonstrated power over nature, and even raised the dead. These miracles were performed in the open and served to validate his claims (Acts 2:22). Jesus told His listeners that if they did not believe His words, they should believe His works (John 10: 37-38).

Jesus performed many miracles in His ministry,

a fact which was never questioned by His enemies. The Council of Pharisees met not to decide whether or not Jesus had performed any miracles but rather, how they could stop Him from doing any more. Because they could not deny His incredible miracles, they said that He performed such miracles by the power of Satan (Mark 3:22). The enemies of Jesus never tried to expose Him as a clever magician or publicly explain how He was able to do His magic tricks.

The miracles of Jesus were given to be "catalysts" for faith; however, many unbelievers hold them to be "obstacles" hindering faith. Today's scientific world view does not embrace supernatural explanations. This is why some have sought to explain the miracles of Jesus away with naturalistic explanations. Some theologians have even gone so far as to accept Jesus as divine but reject the miraculous stories about Jesus. This is inconsistent with the eyewitness testimonies given about the life of Jesus. Any portrayal of Jesus other than as the miraculous Christ is a myth. Therefore, a denial that Jesus performed any miracles is tantamount to denying that Jesus is the Christ.

The denial of miracles stems from an anti-theism bias. Miracles are discredited by skeptics because they assume that God does not exist. They explain miracles in terms of naturalistic explanations. However, the kind of miracles Jesus worked could not be performed by magicians, nor were the miracles believed because the witnesses were pre-scientific people. The healings of Jesus could not have been staged, nor could His resurrection from the dead. Such miracles would still merit amazement in our modern scientific community.

Logically, if God exists, then miracles are possible. If this is so, then the question is not, "Can miracles occur?" but, "Have miracles occurred?" This is why Jesus came performing miracles — to prove that He was from God. Throughout the miracle-laden ministry of Jesus, neither friend nor foe could dispute the reality of His miracles. Nicodemus, the Pharisee, confessed that no one could do the signs that Jesus performed except by the power of God (John 3:2). Thus, the historically documented miracles of Jesus point to the undeniable fact that He is God.

THE EVIDENCE OF THE VIRGIN BIRTH

Seven hundred years before Jesus was born, Isaiah prophesied, "Therefore the Lord Himself will give you a sign: Behold, the virgin shall conceive and bear a Son, and shall call his name Immanuel" (Isa. 7:14). "Immanuel" means "God with us." Isaiah predicted that one of the major "signs" of the anticipated Saviour would be His coming by means of a virgin birth.

Though called "the virgin birth," Jesus' birth could better be referred to as the "virgin conception." Both Matthew and Luke provide detailed accounts of the virgin birth. The Bible teaches that Jesus was conceived in Mary's womb by the power of the Holy Spirit previous to any sexual relations. God chose to enter this world through a biological miracle referred to as the "incarnation," which literally means "becoming in flesh."

Jesus was not a new being, but an already existing divine being who actually became a man. Jesus was more than a mere man who taught us about God. He is the God-man who brought salvation to men.

Before the birth of Jesus, the angel announced to Joseph, "And she shall bring forth a Son; and you shall call his name Jesus: for he will save his people from their sins" (Matt. 1:21). The name "Jesus" means "Jehovah is salvation." The mission of the Messiah prophetically and theologically required a miraculous birth. Jesus appeared in history as the God-man who was free from sin. Jesus did not inherit a sin nature from His parents, but the virgin birth makes possible the entrance of a sinless Son of God.

Many deny the virgin birth on the grounds that it is biologically impossible. But, that is the whole point; it is impossible! That is precisely what makes the virgin birth a "sign." If it was not miraculous, it would not be a "sign." Anyone who can believe that God created the world, should have no difficulty in the possibility believing in a miraculous birth. The virgin birth is no more difficult a miracle than any of the other miracles found in the Bible.

The virgin birth is only part of the entire miracle of the incarnation. One must also ponder the divine truth of "how" God could become a man. It would be more difficult to believe that God became a man by the natural reproductive process of humans, than to believe that Jesus was supernaturally conceived. Hence, the virgin birth is the logical corollary of the incarnation.

To deny the miracle of the virgin birth comes suspiciously close to denying that God exists. As stated earlier, if God exists, then believing in miracles is not a problem. The doctrine of the virgin birth has been attacked since the third century largely by critics who have challenged the deity of Jesus. Acceptance of the doctrine of the virgin birth logically entails an acceptance of the deity of Christ. This is why the doctrine of the virgin birth was essential to the message of the Early Church that Jesus was God. This is evidenced by the importance of doctrinal creeds of the Early Church.

Whereas the early attacks on the virgin birth came from outside the Church, today many inside the Church challenge this biblical teaching. The liberal viewpoint holds that the virgin birth is a stumbling block to accepting Christianity. Such teachers have taught that the virgin birth does not affect any of the vital parts of Christianity and is not essential to the plan of salvation. However, denying the virgin birth compromises the doctrine of the incarnation and the authority of the Bible. The Bible asserts importance of the virgin birth as an aid and indicator of knowing that Jesus is the long-awaited Messiah.

In truth, it is not likely that teaching of the virgin birth would ever suddenly thrust hearers into unbelief, but rather, such unbelief is generated by a heart already predisposed to deny the existence of God. In other words, the unbelief was already present when the person was exposed to this messianic "sign." The witnesses of the virgin birth in the first century were not caused to stumble but were driven to the firm conviction that Jesus was the Messiah. No wonder Ignatius, an Early Church bishop who was martyred around 117, said that the virgin birth was one of the "mysteries to be shouted about."[2] The virgin birth is one of the supreme signs that Jesus is God.

THE EVIDENCE OF DIVINE ATTRIBUTES

Jesus is not just an extraordinary human — He is God. The deity of Christ is explicitly taught in the Scriptures. The writers of the New Testament on many occasions directly refer to Jesus as God (Titus 2:13; John 14:9; Rom. 9:5; John 1:1; John 20:28). The enemies of Jesus also understood that this was the claim of Jesus as they accused Him of blasphemy (John 10:33).

The claim of Jesus to be God was not the raving of a mad lunatic; there is compelling evidence that what He claimed was true. Jesus possesses all the attributes of God, even though He took the form of a human body. Colossians 2:9 states that "for in him dwells all the fullness of the Godhead bodily." Consider the attributes of Jesus on the next page.

No other religious leader has ever demonstrated such powerful attributes in his life. Nor has any other religious leader substantiated the claim to be God. Jesus told His disciples that those who had seen Him had actually seen God (John 14:9). The message of the Bible centers around the truth that a right relationship with God is only found in a relationship with Jesus Christ (John 14:6). When a person believes in Jesus, he/she is believing in God (John 12:44).

JESUS' ATTRIBUTES OF DEITY

CHARACTERISTIC	SCRIPTURE
Preexistence	John 8:58
Creator of the universe	Heb. 1:2
Sinless	2 Cor. 5:21
Forgives sins	Mark 2:5
Power over nature	Mark 4:41
Raise the dead	John 11:1-44
Power over disease	John 9:25-32
Resurrection	1 Cor. 15:3-5
Eternal	Rev. 1:8; Rev. 22:13
Holy	John 6:69
Omnipresent	Matt. 28:20
Omnipotent	Matt. 28:18
Omniscient	John 16:30
Immutable	Heb. 13:8
Sustainer of creation	Heb. 1:3; Col. 1:17
Brings salvation	1 John 4:14
Accepts worship	John 9:38
Object of prayer	Acts 7:59
Universal judge	Matt. 25:31-46

THE EVIDENCE OF THE TRILEMMA ARGUMENT

Many non-Christians who have difficulty accepting that Jesus is God have no trouble professing that Jesus was a great moral teacher. However, this position is not only illogical but impossible. Jesus claimed to be divine, nothing less. If Jesus was not God, He would be far less than just a great, moral teacher; He would be deluded, or a deceiver. There would be nothing great about the teaching of a man who merely pretended to be God. His teachings, if believed, would steer people away from the truth. Jesus cannot be regarded as a great teacher, but not divine. There are only three options as to who Jesus was in light of His claims.

POSSIBILITIES AS TO THE IDENTITY OF JESUS	
IDENTITY	IMPLICATIONS
1. Deity	His message should be believed and trusted.
2. Deceiver	His message is that of a false, religious teacher. Jesus tricked people into following him.
3. Deluded	Jesus was simply a mentally ill person who believed that he was really God.

Let us examine all three.

First: Was Jesus a Deceiver?

This option holds that Jesus was a liar and willfully deceived people about religious truth. Jesus certainly could not be regarded as a great, moral teacher if He were found to be a pathological liar. Jesus would be a hypocrite of the highest order, instructing His followers in honesty and virtue while He lived out a religious deception. Such a person would necessary be demonically evil, leading multitudes from the true path of salvation into eternal damnation.

Very few have ever accused Jesus of being a liar because this is not consistent with what is known about the life of Jesus. A deceiver would not have lived such a selfless, virtuous, dignified life. Jesus' entire life was spent teaching and ministering to people. No person has ever been judged as honest and morally sound as Jesus of Nazareth.

The notion of Jesus willfully perpetuating a religious deception makes no sense. What would Jesus have to gain by such a lie? He never tried to profit financially as is usually the primary motive of religious deceivers. Moreover, if Jesus had been a religious deceiver, He certainly would have changed His story in the face of an impending death. It is inconceivable that such a deceiver would have centered His ministry around a sacrificial death. Jesus was far too sincere and selfless to have been a deceiver.

Second: Could Jesus Have Been Deluded?

Was Jesus merely a sincere person who mistakenly thought He was God? We have a word which describes such people today — mentally ill. Asylums abound with persons who believe they are divine, their illness is obvious, they are usually incoherent and prone to schizophrenia. Such people live in an isolated world of fantasy, often incapable of relations with others.

Jesus never displayed such characteristics. In Jesus, we find one of the greatest intellects in all of history having total control of His mind and actions. His words not only had a profound influence of the people of His day, but they also continue to improve the lives of men and women today. Jesus was never confused by His critics but gave profound answers which silenced the wisest men of His day. The enemies of Jesus cowered in the face of His superior wisdom and knowledge. Such a man does not fit the psychological profile of a deluded person.

Last: Is Jesus Diety?

Jesus was not a madman claiming to be God; He had the credentials to back up His claim. There is sufficient evidence to substantiate that Jesus is divine. If you agree that Jesus was neither a deceiver nor deluded, then the only alternative left is that Jesus is deity.

Which option do you believe is correct? Some have opted to ignore this question, but this is the most important question in history. You cannot remain neutral about this issue because the stakes are eternal life. Do you believe that Jesus is God? Jesus emphatically declared, "If you do not believe that I am he, you will die in your sins" (John 8:24). Complimenting Jesus as a great, moral teacher is not enough — you must believe in Jesus as God. If you have not believed in Jesus Christ, you are still in your sins. Man is judged not only because of sin, but also for rejecting the witness of Jesus Christ. Jesus declared, "He who believes in him is not condemned; but he who does not believe is condemned already, because he has not believed in the name of the only begotten Son of God" (John 3:18).

What reason have atheists for saying that we cannot rise again? Which is the more difficult, to be born, or to rise again? That what has never been, should be, or that what has been, should be again? Is it more difficult to come into being than to return to it?

Blaise Pascal

Pensees, XXIV

4

Jesus Rose from the Dead

J esus came to earth to save mankind from penalty, power, and the presence of sin. Jesus is the Saviour of the human race. The image of Saviour is not unlike that of the lifeguard. The job of the lifeguard is to save drowning people. To qualify as a lifeguard, one must be "willing" and "able" to save someone from drowning.

In the same manner, man is drowning in sin. The Bible tells us that man will die physically because of sin, but sin also causes spiritual separation from God (Rom. 6:23). To die in one's sins is to be separated from God for eternity. This everlasting separation is what the Bible calls the second death (Rev. 2:11). Throughout history, various religious leaders have sought to assume the role of the religious lifeguard in order to help those drowning in sin, though they themselves were drowning with the rest of humanity. Unfortunately, being mere men, these religious leaders did not have the ability to qualify as Saviour.

Jesus Christ came to earth as creation's cosmic lifeguard to save mankind from the second death. To be a Saviour presupposes that one has the ability to save. Thus, how do we know that Jesus could do what He said he could do? What makes Jesus different from all other religious leaders? The answer is found in the tomb of Jesus of Nazareth — it has no tenant. The bones of all other dead religious leaders may be found buried here on earth; however, the tomb of Jesus remains empty. A dead lifeguard can save no one. Christianity does not ask its followers to follow a dead religious leader, but to follow a resurrected Christ. This was the message of the Early Church. The early Christians preached the gospel or "good news" of the resurrection of Jesus Christ.

DEFINING THE CONCEPT

Many have misunderstood what the Resurrection is and what it means. The Resurrection is not reincarnation. Jesus' soul did not pass on to another body after death. He had the same body that was placed in the tomb. Neither was Jesus merely resuscitated. People who are resuscitated later die. Near-

DEFINITIONS	
CONCEPT	**MEANING**
Resuscitation	Vital signs stop then restart
Reincarnation	Soul passes to another body at death
Resurrection	Physical body is made incorruptible

death experiences are not permanent. That is why these people may receive brief notoriety but are ultimately forgotten. Jesus, on the other hand, was raised with an incorruptible body which could never again be subject to the powers of death. The resurrection of Jesus is permanent.

THE HISTORICAL FACTS

While not everyone believes in the actual resurrection of Christ, there are many reported facts concerning the Resurrection which are conceded by virtually all critical scholars. Though many deny the Christian interpretation of the Resurrection, the majority of scholars acknowledge the historicity of the following facts:

1. Jesus of Nazareth died by means of crucifixion.

2. Jesus' body was placed in a guarded tomb.

3. The disciples were shattered that their Messiah had died. They lost all hope and did not expect a Resurrection.

4. The tomb of Jesus was found empty on the third day.

5. Eyewitnesses reported the bodily appearance of Jesus on several occasions.

6. The shattered faith of the disciples was radically transformed into a bold belief in the Resurrection. The disciples from this point willingly sacrificed their lives for the cause of Christianity.

7. The proclamation of the Early Church was unapologetically the Resurrection of Jesus Christ. This preaching began in Jerusalem where Jesus was crucified.

8. The Christian Church sprang from news of the Resurrection. Sunday became the featured day of worship.

9. Jesus appeared to James and to Paul, both of whom experienced conversion as a result of their encounters with the risen Christ.

There are certainly more facts than these, but any theory of the Resurrection must account for these facts. Many naturalistic theories have been proposed which have tried to explain away the Resurrection but do not harmonize with the historical data.

THE HISTORICAL SIGNIFICANCE

The explanation that Jesus rose from the dead best explains the body of historical evidence. This greatest miracle of the Bible comes complete with convincing historical data. Hence, the Resurrection can be judged in the same way as any other historical event. The reality of the Resurrection is not merely a question of theology nor philosophy, but one of history. The Resurrection would not be credible without being historical.

The Resurrection must not be confused with the category of myth. The life and ministry of Jesus Christ clearly belongs within the realm of history. History tells us very much about Jesus. We know where He was born, the time that He lived, and where He spent most of His life. Every encyclopedia and history of the ancient world records the fact of Jesus' existence. More information exists about His death than any other person in the ancient world. The secular writings of His age tell us that his contemporaries — such as Herod the Great, Pontius Pilate, Felix, Festus, Tiberias, Caesar, Herod Agrippa, and many others — were historical people.

The resurrection of Jesus Christ is one of the most certain facts of all of history. Professor Thomas Arnold, former history professor at Oxford, stated, "I have been used for many years to study the histories of other times, and to examine and weigh the evidence of those who have written about them, and I know of no one fact in the history of mankind which is proved by better and fuller evidence of every sort to the understanding of a fair inquirer, than the great sign which God has given us that Christ died and rose again from the dead."[1]

The variety of testimony and other evidences makes the Resurrection the greatest attested miracle ever documented in history.

THE RESURRECTION CHALLENGE

The Resurrection stands not only as one of the most certain events in history, but it remains and will continue to be, by far, the most important event of all history. If the Resurrection is true, then there is a God, and Jesus is Saviour of the world.

Does it really matter if the Resurrection actually happened? Of course! Why? Because the Resurrection is the key to Christianity. If the Resurrection is not true, the Bible says that Christians would be great fools (1 Cor. 15:14-19). If the Resurrection were proved to be false, it could be shown that Christianity is not the ultimate truth for mankind. Without the claim of the Resurrection, Christianity could never survive the attacks of its critics.

The Resurrection is the key to evaluating the claims of Jesus Christ. Many have sought to know if Jesus is truly God and not found the answer. Perhaps this is because they have been asking the wrong questions. The key to getting the right answers is asking the correct questions. The answer to the question, "Is Jesus God?" may best be answered in the question, "Did Jesus rise from the dead?" The Resurrection is the starting point for any investigation as to the identity of Jesus of Nazareth.

If it is shown that Jesus did rise from the dead, then the claims of Christ are validated. One of the main purposes of the Resurrection is that it serves as a "sign" to confirm to us that what Jesus said was true. Thus, if Jesus was raised from the dead, then He truly is the only way of salvation (John 14:6). The Resurrection is God's "amen" that Jesus is His chosen way of salvation. Once it is seen that the

Resurrection is true, one does not need to examine the claims of other religious leaders — for they are of necessity false. If Christ is truly risen, no further search is necessary.

The question of the Resurrection must be approached as any other historical question. Have you ever conducted this type of investigation? If you became convinced the Resurrection actually took place, would you become a Christian?

Many skeptics have taken "The Resurrection Challenge" and sought to investigate if Jesus really rose from the dead. Many of these skeptics were won over to Christianity as a result of their search. Many famous, legal experts — such as Simon Greenleaf and Frank Morrison — changed their mind as a result of weighing the evidence. Morrison set out to write a book discrediting Christianity. He instead wrote *Who Moved the Stone*, which powerfully argues the evidence for the resurrection of Jesus Christ.

The evidence for the Resurrection is powerful and compelling. Lord Darling, former Chief Justice of England, concluded, "In its favour as a living truth there exists such overwhelming evidence, positive and negative, factual and circumstantial, that no intelligent jury in the world could fail to bring in a verdict that the resurrection story is true."[2] Belief in the Resurrection is not a leap into the dark, but rather a truth which is based on solid historical evidence.

THE RESURRECTION EVIDENCES

When this evidence is examined without bias,

there is sufficient evidence to merit belief. To disbelieve the Resurrection accounts, one must deliberately ignore the rules of evidence used in all other areas of historical inquiry. Please examine the following evidences honestly and openly and you also can experience the miracle and power of the resurrection of Jesus Christ.

The Evidence from Prophecy

The Resurrection was not a surprise nor a last minute addition to the new religion of Christianity. The Resurrection was prophesied of in the Old Testament (see Gen. 3:15; Ps. 2:7; Ps. 16:9-11; Ps. 22:14-15; Ps. 40:1-3; Ps. 110:1; Isa. 53:9-12; Hosea 5 and 6; Zech. 12:10). Paul tells us in 1 Corinthians 15:3-4, "For I delivered unto you first of all that which I also received: that Christ died for our sins according to the Scriptures, and that he was buried, and that he rose again the third day according to the Scriptures."

Jesus also repeatedly predicted His death and subsequent resurrection (see Matt. 12:38-42; Matt. 16:21; Matt. 17:9; Matt. 17:23; Matt. 20:19; Mark 14:28; Luke 9:22; John 2:19). Jesus frequently asserted that He would rise from the dead to validate His claims and teachings. To say that Jesus stressed the importance of the Resurrection is an understatement.

Jesus staked His entire ministry on the single fact that He would rise from the dead. Why would Jesus risk destroying the entire religious movement of Christianity by giving a false prophecy? Jesus displayed incredible confidence that He would die and in three days rise from the dead. Jesus indicated that this was to be a supernatural "sign" that He really was the Messiah.

Such a claim would be foolish unless Jesus was 100 percent sure He could really rise from the dead. If someone made such a claim today, they would be carried away to a mental institution. Such an original claim cannot be found falling from the lips of any other great religious leader.

But the claim of Jesus rising from the dead is totally consistent with His character and who He claimed to be. Jesus staked His entire claim to messiahship on His ability to rise from the dead. He urged people to make their decision based on this evidence. If He did not rise, He would have been viewed as one of the biggest fools of all history.

Is this not the kind of hard proof that the human mind longs to hold on to? What other religious leader ever performed historical miracles like Jesus did? What other religion has such an astounding test of authenticity? If a person will not believe after being convinced of the evidence of the Resurrection, he/she will not likely believe any other evidence that might be presented.

The Evidence of the Empty Tomb

The empty tomb alone does not prove that the Resurrection occurred, but if Jesus did rise from the dead, the empty tomb is a logical corollary. All four gospels record the fact of the empty tomb (Matt. 28:1-10; Mark 16:6; Luke 24:1-11; John 20:1-10). Though the empty tomb is not in and of itself proof of the Resurrection, it is consistent with the cumulative evidence supporting a resurrection. The fact of the empty tomb is so well-established that it is recognized even by those who have spurious theories on the Resurrection. Even the enemies of Jesus acknowledged the empty tomb following the crucifixion. There has never been any evidence brought to bear which can disprove it.

One of the strongest evidences for the empty tomb lies in the burial of Jesus. The burial of Jesus is one of the best-established facts about Jesus. Jesus was buried by Joseph of Arimathea, who was a member of the Sanhedrin. Had the early Christians made up the account of the burial, they could not have been successful in spreading a false story that one of the Sanhedrin buried Jesus. If the burial were a fictitious story, it would have been disproved very quickly. The burial account is a well-known Christian tradition which was widely spread by the first disciples (1 Cor. 15:3-5). Thus, if the burial is true, so is the account of the empty tomb.

Strong evidence supports an empty tomb in light of the fact that the tomb of Jesus was never venerated. Tomb veneration involves worshipers going to the tomb of a religious leader to engage in worship. This practice exists today and was frequently practiced in Jesus day. However, the tomb of Jesus never became a place of veneration as the tombs of other famous prophets. Why? Jesus was not there!

The empty tomb also served as a "sign" that something miraculous had happened. The tomb of Jesus was not completely empty. The graveclothes were still there. In Eastern burials the body was tightly wrapped with linen strips about one foot wide. In between these layers were spices and gummy substances, totaling about 100 pounds which would help bind everything together (John 19:39-40).

When the witnesses arrived at the empty tomb, they saw something incredible. They saw the graveclothes empty and undisturbed yet the body of Jesus was gone. The graveclothes were still in the shape of the body with the empty napkin exactly preserved. Understand that no graverobbers could ever accomplish such a feat by stripping away the glued cloth and shaping them back in the appearance of a body.

This sight had an incredible effect. When the disciple John looked into the tomb, "he saw and believed" (John 20:8). It was as though the body of Jesus had vaporized. This was no resuscitation; something supernatural had occurred. It could be seen that the body of Jesus passed through the graveclothes. This remains consistent with the eyewitness appearances of the resurrected body of Jesus which could appear and disappear at will (Luke 24:15-36; John 20:19-26).

The graveclothes served as "visual evidence" that death could not hold Jesus. This sight alone caused the disciples' doubts to flee and give way to belief. The empty tomb not only testified that Jesus was gone, it produced the effect that Jesus had indeed rose from the dead.

The Evidence from Eyewitnesses

If Jesus' body was not in the grave, where was it? Eyewitnesses began to report encounters with the risen Christ immediately after finding the tomb empty. These appearances explain why the tomb was empty — Jesus was alive! The empty tomb was only the beginning. Jesus began to appear to many people.

The appearances of Jesus lasted for over 40 days until the time of His ascension. Jesus appeared to individuals, small groups, and large groups. He appeared to a variety of people in various locations. Acts 1:3 also indicates many unrecorded appearances during the 40 days of appearances.

These eyewitness reports were published during the lifetimes of those who were alive during the Resurrection. This gives credibility to the authenticity of these reports. Paul realized this and challenged anyone who doubted the Resurrection to go and question the eyewitnesses, seeing as a majority of them were still alive (1 Cor. 15:6).

The eyewitness sightings created dynamic faith in the hearts of those who saw. Those who became convinced by Jesus of His resurrection never wavered in their belief again. This was the purpose of Jesus' resurrection appearances. Jesus wished to impart an unshakable faith upon which He could found a solid Church which would be impervious to the attacks of persecution.

The Evidence of the
Transformation of the Disciples

All history is based upon testimony. Testimony gives us the facts of what has transpired in the past. Hence, the question must be asked, "How do we know that the eyewitnesses of the Resurrection told

POST-RESURRECTION APPEARANCES		
EYEWITNESS	**LOCATION**	**REFERENCES**
Mary Magdalene	Sepulchre	John 20:11
Other women	Returning from Sepulchre	Matt. 28:1-10
Peter	Unknown	Luke 24:34
Cleopas and another	Road to Emmaus	Mark 16:12-13
Ten Apostles	Meal at Easter	Luke 24:36-40
Thomas and other Apostles	House	John 20:26-30
Seven disciples	Sea of Tiberias	John 21:1-23
To five hundred people	Galilee	1 Cor. 15:6
Apostles	Mount of Olives	Mark 16:19
James	Unknown	1 Cor. 15:7
Paul	Damascus Road	Acts 9:1-22
John	Isle of Patmos	Rev.1:10-19

the truth?" One of the most powerful evidences that eyewitnesses had seen the risen Christ was seen in their remarkable transformations.

Following the arrest of Jesus, the disciples all hid in fear of being put to death. The disciples met in secret following the crucifixion for fear of the Jews (John 20:19). Peter denied Jesus three times in order to save his own life (Mark 14:66-72). But something happened which would completely reverse the attitudes of the disciples. The disciples suddenly began to preach the Resurrection without fear of punishment or death. At Pentecost, Peter boldly preaches to thousands about the resurrection of Jesus, and with reckless abandon, the disciples proclaimed the Easter truth in the face of those responsible for the crucifixion of Jesus (Acts 2:23-24).

Their preaching, of course, brought immediate persecution, suffering, and death. Yet, these eyewitnesses willingly gave their lives for the message they knew to be true. A majority of the Apostles died in a violent manner because of their faith in Christ. However, not even one Apostle renounced Christ under the pressure of death. They authenticated their sincerity with their own blood. These men willingly died in order to validate the sincerity of their belief.

Sincerity does not prove the truth, but it proves something very important in the Resurrection story. If the Resurrection was a fraud, it would have had to have originated with the disciples. The disciples could have never been deceived into thinking Jesus rose from the dead if He really did not. If the Resurrection was a lie, they not only would have known it, they would have been its conspirators.

Lies are usually told for some kind of profit or advantage. The disciples had absolutely nothing to gain by proclaiming such a monumental lie in the face of a hostile audience. If the Resurrection was a lie, such selfish men would have surely spread their teachings covertly thus avoiding the possibility of death. It would have been foolish to suffer such horrible deaths based upon a fabrication. How could their religion of truth originate from a lie? It is inconceivable to believe that rational people would hold to such fantasy all the way unto death.

These men had everything to lose and nothing to gain by lying about the Resurrection. The Resurrection had to have been true for the Apostles to so daringly proclaim this truth in the face of their enemies. They bet their very lives that the Resurrection was true. Even death could not make them change their story. Death has an incredible way of bringing the truth out. The early Christian writer Tertullian wrote that "no man would be willing to die unless he knew he had the truth."[3]

For its first 300 years, the Church endured the menace of persecution. Through nine different periods of persecution, the early Christians steadfastly held to the truth that Jesus rose from the dead.

It is certain that had not these Christians so fervently maintained their belief in the resurrection, Christianity would have ended with the death of Jesus. They believed unto death that Jesus rose from the dead and was the Saviour.

Many people have died for a cause they believed was true even though it was false; however, no one ever eagerly dies for a cause knowing it to be false. Christianity could have never endured had these first Christians not believed in the Resurrection.

PERSECUTION IN THE EARLY CHURCH

PERSECUTOR	DATE	MAJOR MARTYR
Jews	A.D. 33-A.D. 64	Stephen
Nero	A.D. 64-A.D. 68	Peter
Domitian	A.D. 81-A.D. 96	Flavius Clemons
Trajan	A.D. 98-A.D. 117	Polycarp
Septimius Severus	A.D. 193-A.D. 211	Clement of Alexandria
Decius	A.D. 249-A.D. 251	Novatian
Valerian	A.D. 253-A.D. 260	Cyprian
Diocletion	A.D. 303-A.D. 313	Crispina of Numidia

The tenacity of these early eyewitnesses in the face of death testifies to the truth that the Resurrection must have occurred.

The Evidence of Jesus Being Worshiped as God

Have you ever seen anyone rise from the dead? It is difficult to understand how an ordinary human being could rise from the dead. But history teaches us Jesus rose from the dead. Many cannot accept this well-documented fact of history. Much of the problem lies in fully understanding who Jesus is. He is not an ordinary human being. In fact, once one understands who Jesus really is, one would not be able to understand why Jesus would not be able to rise from the dead! Luke wrote that Jesus was "who God raised up, having loosed the pains of death, because it was not possible that he should be held by it" (Acts 2:24). There is a vast difference between an ordinary person rising from the dead and Jesus rising from the dead.

The disciples constantly struggled trying to comprehend the divine nature of Jesus. Only over a gradual period of time did the disciples fully understand the teachings of Jesus concerning His deity. The Resurrection pulled it all together for the struggling disciples. Thomas, upon seeing and touching the resurrected Jesus, declared, "My Lord and my God" (John 20:28). Jesus did not rebuke him but accepted this confession of deity.

Jesus was never venerated as a dead teacher, but was worshipped as the living God. The first Christians instinctively worshiped Jesus and directed their prayers to him. This behavior was totally inappropriate if Jesus was dead. The Resurrection helped to substantiate who Jesus is. Paul wrote that Jesus was "declared to be the Son of God with power according to the Spirit of holiness, by the resurrection from the dead" (Rom. 1:4). From the time of the Resurrection on, Jesus was unapologetically worshiped as God by the newly established Christian Church.

The Evidence of the Church

The Resurrection was not a concept invented by the Church but an event. It is not a philosophy that evolved but a fact that occurred. It is impossible to explain the remarkable birth of the Church without the truth of the Resurrection. There is no other logical cause which can explain what established Christianity. No delusion could have achieved the effects that were produced by Christianity. Without a resurrection, a handful of cowardly men could have never changed the world.

The Christian Church arose from the preaching of the Resurrection. Luke wrote that the Apostles "with great power the Apostles gave witness to the resurrection of the Lord Jesus" (Acts 4:33). It was not the teaching of Jesus that was the centerpiece of early Christian proclamation; rather, it was the message that the crucified Messiah was now alive. This became the heart of all Christian worship.

The Church can be historically traced back to A.D. 30 in Jerusalem. At this time Sunday replaced the Sabbath as a day of worship. This Sunday celebration came to be known as the Lord's Day and was celebrated once a week as a weekly reminder of the Resurrection. How could one account for such a shift had the Resurrection not taken place?

One cannot read a history of the world without speaking of the vast scope and prominence of the Church. The Church and its message of a resurrected Christ have been a powerful reality for over 19 centuries. What is the explanation for this incredible organization which transformed the world? The only possible explanation is the one provided by the Church — Jesus is alive.

Cambridge scholar C. F. D. Moule wrote, "If the coming into existence of the Nazarenes, a great phenomenon undeniably attested by the New Testament, rips a great hole in history, a hole the size of the Resurrection, what does the secular historian propose to stop it up with?"[4] Many such attempts have been made to explain away the Resurrection, and all have miserably failed.

OBJECTIONS TO THE RESURRECTION

The Resurrection has withstood the attacks of the greatest minds in history. Through all the centuries of the Church, only a few theories have been proposed to refute the truth of the Resurrection. However, each of these theories takes more faith to believe than the Resurrection itself. Clearly one of the best ways to see the truth of the Resurrection is to examine the alternatives and see how preposterous they are.

The Myth Theory

Some would argue that the account of the Resurrection is simply a myth. However, this theory is not plausible in that the Resurrection account has no earmarks of mythology. Almost no one holds to this theory, primarily because "historical research has not produced any convincing evidence that the event of Jesus' resurrection fits the model of myth, pure legend, or delusion."[5]

The New Testament treats the Resurrection as a definite historical event. It would have been impossible for the Resurrection to have been a myth. The short amount of time between the Resurrection and the gospel narratives does not allow sufficient time for a legend to develop. Further, the Church developed in the same exact geographical location where the Resurrection event occurred. Had the disciples fabricated their facts, other eyewitnesses could have refuted their embellishment. It would have been easy for anyone to investigate the accuracy of their story.

Myths, characterized by exaggeration and embellishment, are not found in the gospels. In fact, just the opposite is the case. The gospels record that the empty tomb was first discovered by women. Women at this time held low social status and did not even qualify to be legal witnesses. Josephus wrote, "From women let no evidence be accepted, because of the levity and temerity of their sex."[6] If the account was truly a legend, then male disciples would have been the ones to make the Resurrection discovery. Explaining the Resurrection away as myth does not coincide with the core facts of crucifixion and death of Jesus of Nazareth. Only the Christian account of the Resurrection fits all the facts.

The Hallucination Theory

This theory holds that those who were witnesses of the Resurrection merely thought they saw
Jesus. Those who hold to the hallucination theory
ignore what is known about those who hallucinate.
Usually only the mentally ill have hallucinations,
and such occurrences are personal and are linked to
the person's past. It is statistically unlikely that two
people could have the same hallucination.

The risen Christ appeared to groups of people,
some as large as 500. They reported seeing and
eating with Jesus for 40 days. Hallucinations do not
eat and they usually occur repeatedly over a long
period of time. The disciples did not continue to see
Jesus after He ascended to heaven at the end of the
40 days.

If the disciples were merely victims of a mass
illusion, then where was the body of Jesus? The site
of their preaching was only a few minutes from the
tomb of Jesus. If they were hallucinating, someone
could have taken them to the tomb of Jesus and
displayed the body. If the resurrection was only
hallucination, why did the guards report the body
missing, and what would one make of the actions of
the high priests? The hallucination theory does not
fit the facts.

The Wrong Tomb Theory

This theory, first proposed by Kirsopp Lake in
1907, suggests that the women lost their way to the
tomb on Sunday morning and went to the wrong
tomb. This theory is easily dismissed. First, when
the women arrived, the sun was already up (Mark

16:2). It is doubtful they could have gone to the wrong tomb seeing as they had just seen the body of Jesus there 36 hours earlier (Mark 15:47).

Further, it could not have been the wrong tomb because when they told others, they also came to the tomb and saw that it was empty, and the graveclothes of Jesus were still intact inside (John 20:4-6). The disciples, Jesus, Roman guards, and the owner of the tomb all unanimously conceded that it was the correct tomb.

The Stolen Body Theory

This was the first explanation ever given. When the Roman guards were left guarding an empty tomb, they knew they could be put to death for not having the body of Jesus. Instead of going back to Pilate, who likely would have enforced the law and had them killed, they went to the Jewish high priests. The Jewish leaders bribed the guards to say that the disciples stole the body while they were sleeping (Matt. 28:13).

This explanation is really quite humorous. If the guards were sleeping, how would they know if the disciples were the thieves? Did they leave a business card behind? How could one sleep through the moving of a two-ton stone? Such testimony would be laughed out of court. The authorities knew full well that the disciples did not take the body or else they would have arrested, questioned, and executed the disciples. If there was any evidence of a theft they could have stopped Christianity dead in its tracks.

The disciples were honest men whose character

does not fit that of thieves. Why would a thief steal the body and then openly walk around with a death warrant hanging over his head? They had no motive for stealing the body of Jesus. They could not profit financially or any other way from such an endeavor. When they were ultimately arrested and tortured, they did not confess to such a theft.

The Jewish leaders nor the Romans had any motive for removing the body of Jesus. In fact, they went to great lengths to insure that the body would not be stolen. When the disciples began to preach the Resurrection, if the authorities had possession of the body, they would have only had to display the corpse to end the birth of Christianity. But they could not produce the corpse because they did not have Jesus' body. Only the fact of the Resurrection accounts for all of the facts.

The Swoon Theory

This theory, proposed by H. E. G. Paulus in 1828, holds that Jesus did not actually die on the cross. Paulus asserted that when the soldier thrust the spear into Jesus, he missed the heart and pierced a vein.

Medical doctors of the 19th century believed that bleeding someone could help them recover faster. Paulus proposed that the loss of blood helped Jesus recover from His brush with death. Jesus then appeared to several of His disciples who being ignorant, assumed that He had come back from the dead. After 40 days, Jesus eventually died from His wounds and the body was never found. This theory was widespread among 18th century rationalists who were deliberately looking for a reason not to believe. However, there is simply no evidence that Jesus swooned.

The facts confirm that Jesus died. A spear was thrust into Jesus' side to confirm that He was dead. Out poured blood and water. The separation of blood from serum is one of the surest medical evidences that death has occurred. The soldiers were so positive of Jesus' death that they did not break His legs. Only after Pilate received an official report of Jesus' death would he release the body. Jesus was dead.

The swoon theory requires an unbelievable amount of faith. It is difficult to understand how a half-dead man, beaten beyond recognition, could convince others He had risen from the dead. How could a beaten man in need of medical attention trick a trained Roman execution squad, escape from heavy wrappings, move a two-ton stone, overcome the soldiers at the tomb, walk 14 miles to Emmaus, and then convince His disciples He was the mighty conqueror of death? How could a dying man, too weak to even have carried His own cross, inspire the disciples to unshakable boldness and courage in the face of death? A mere resuscitation would have only weakened the faith of the disciples.

A modern version of the swoon theory was proposed in 1965 by Hugh Schoenfield in his work *The Passover Plot*. Schoenfield theorized that Jesus set out to arrange His life so as to fulfill many messianic prophecies. By means of a drug, He falsified His death on the cross. His fellow conspirator, Joseph of Arimathea, was to take Jesus' body to a tomb where He could later be revived. The plan was ruined by a Roman soldier who thrust a spear into Jesus' side from which He died. Later an unknown man was mistaken for Jesus on several occasions which led the disciples to believe that Jesus had returned from the dead.

It is easily seen that neither of the swoon theories can be harmonized with the facts. Such theories are the inventions of minds desperate not to believe. The evidence for the resurrection is clearly enough to convince any open-minded inquirer. To disbelieve the Resurrection, one must deliberately disregard the rules used everywhere else in history.

No plausible naturalistic explanation for the Resurrection exists. Those who deny the Resurrection have no solid reason for doing so. You have just read the leading naturalistic explanations of the Resurrection and seen that they are found wanting. Time and time again critics have tried to put to rest the claim of the Resurrection, but just cannot seem to roll the stone back over the grave. All naturalistic explanations, like the tomb of Jesus, remain empty.

THE MEANING OF THE RESURRECTION

An incredible change occurred in the minds of the disciples. They became convinced Jesus was alive and staked their lives on it. It took nothing less than a miracle to cause this change.

Is not the Resurrection the best explanation of the facts? This is exactly what Jesus said He would do because He was the Son of God. Jesus gave the Resurrection as a "sign" that we could believe He was the truth. Jesus' teachings are verified by a unique, one of a kind, act of God. Jesus' unique teachings are backed up by His unique resurrection from the dead.

No other religious leader can make such a claim. When you understand that Jesus rose from the dead, you have the key to the truth. The Resurrection unveils the true identity of Jesus Christ. The key to Christianity is the Resurrection.

It was this belief in the Resurrection that changed the apostle Paul's life and it can change yours as well. Those who believe in Christ's resurrection and follow Him will also experience the Resurrection in their own lives (1 Cor. 15:12-23). Christ's resurrection has released the power of salvation upon those who surrender their lives to Jesus Christ. The apostle Peter wrote that believers are born again "to a living hope through the resurrection of Jesus Christ from the dead" (1 Peter 1:3).

Just as there are no rational reasons for explaining away the resurrection, there are no acceptable reasons for not becoming a Christian. Jesus died on a cross and was raised on the third day in order that you might obtain His resurrection life. Jesus is not only *willing* to save you, He is *able* to save you.

Truth is incontrovertible. Panic
may resent it; ignorance may
deride it; malice may distort it;
but there it is.

Sir Winston Churchill

5

JESUS IS THE ONLY WAY TO GOD

One of the greatest stumbling blocks in accepting Jesus as Saviour rests in Jesus' claim of exclusivity. Jesus claimed that He is the only way of salvation and that the teachings of different religious leaders are false (John 10:7-13). He promised that those who believe in Him will have eternal life and all who do not believe will suffer the wrath of God (John 3:36). Jesus did not merely claim that His teachings are the truth; he claimed that He is the only truth for mankind (John 14:6).

TRUTH IS TRUTH

Some would argue that while Jesus embodies the truth for some, He may not be necessarily the truth for all. This "pluralistic" view holds that all religions can be subjectively true. But in reality, there is no difference between "religious truth" and "objective truth." Truth is always truth. There is no difference between scientific truth and religious truth.

Truth is something that exists outside of our subjective feelings and thoughts. Truth is never subjectively created but is merely discovered. If something is found to be truth, it is truth for all. Thus, two opposing viewpoints cannot be right; both can be wrong, but both cannot be correct.

RELIGIONS ARE NOT EQUAL

Though other religions have elements of truth, they are mixed with error. All non-Christian religions contain such teachings which stand in direct conflict with the teachings of Christ. This is illogical to say that Christianity is true and yet hold to the validity of other religions. Such a view directly conflicts with the teachings of Jesus Christ. If Jesus is only the Saviour for some people, He lied and is thus the Saviour for no one.

Many people contend that no matter which religion one follows, all religions provide spiritual guidance and basically result in the same outcome. Such statements demonstrate that such persons have no substantial knowledge of world religions because certainly they all differ. In academic circles, some "comparative religion" studies have sought to boil religions down to their lowest common denominator and show them all to be manifestations of the same essence. But this process of reducing leaves each religion different than what its founders intended.

However, something about Christianity sets it apart from religion. Non-Christian religions are man's search for God, but Christianity is the story of God's search for man. All other religions were founded by sinful men, whereas Christianity's founder is God. Other religions are founded upon teachings, Christianity is based upon a person.

Jesus' teachings are based upon who He is. His invitation was not merely to follow His teachings but to follow Him. Jesus did not simply teach about the resurrection and the way of salvation; He said that He *is* the resurrection and the way to God (John 14:6; John 11:25). He is not simply another religious leader who spoke to us in a new way, He is God among us, showing us the way to everlasting life.

Therefore, if the God of the Bible is the true God, then all other gods are non-existent and must not be worshiped. Other religions are not searches for the truth but detours from the truth. Contrary to popular religious thought, religion did not evolve upwards but eroded downwards into various types of religions as man rejected the revelation of God. The world's major religions are based upon earning one's salvation, whereas Christianity is based upon faith in what God has done in Jesus Christ.

Whereas other religions are based upon subjectivity, Christianity is based upon objective facts.

Unlike most other religions, the claims of Christianity can be investigated. Christianity does not solely rest on what Jesus taught but also on what He did. Jesus verified who He was by what He did. If Jesus is who He said He was, then other religious leaders cannot possibly be who they say they are. Logically, if the claims of Christ be false, then He should not even be elevated in the same category as other great religious leaders. But if the claims of Jesus are true, then other religious leaders cannot claim the same authority possessed by Christ, for their teachings are necessarily false.

SINCERITY IS NOT ENOUGH

Some might argue that even if a person's religion is false, what really matters is their sincerity. This notion is based on a false belief that God is pleased by religion. However, the Bible teaches that non-Christian religions are direct rebellion against God.

Sincerity does not determine truth. One can be sincerely convinced of the truth and be sincerely wrong. One can be sincerely right or sincerely wrong. For instance, accidental deaths sometimes occur in the medical field when patients are administered the wrong prescription. Most of these cases involve no malice, but involve medical workers who mistakenly — but sincerely — administered the wrong treatment. Sincerity does not somehow give validity to false religion. Sincerity never adequately substitutes for the truth. Many evil men such as Adolf Hitler were very sincere in their beliefs. God never accepts sincerity for sincerity's sake, but He judges mankind based upon truth, and that truth is Jesus Christ.

CHRISTIANITY IS TOTALLY TRUE

Jesus claimed that Christianity is not the best way to God but the only way to God. Such a claim is either totally true or totally false. Some have sought to give allegiance to Christianity and yet ignore Jesus' claim to be the only Saviour. Critics argue that it is narrow-minded to insist Jesus is the only way to God. But just because Christianity seems narrow does not mean it is untrue. Truth itself is exclusive. If Christianity is true, then we must also accept the teachings of Jesus who demands our total allegiance. If one believes the claims of Jesus to be true, then the issue is settled. Some believe this policy to be cruel and unloving; but, if there are other ways to God, the Bible teaches Christ died in vain (Gal. 2:21). If Christianity truly is the only cure for mankind's problem, would not Christians be cruel and unloving if they did not share the real truth with the world?

THE FATE OF THE UNEVANGELIZED

Some would say, "If Christ is the only way to God, what happens to those who have not heard?" This question is usually a smokescreen posed by those who are trying to rationalize their own rejection of Christ. Such questions sometimes imply that God lacks compassion for imposing his plan of salvation upon mankind. Often such inquirers seem to imply that they are more compassionate than God!

Such questions expose people's lack of knowledge about salvation. These questions assume that people are lost because they have not heard the gospel, but people are actually lost because of their sin of rejection of God. Jesus came to die for people's sin so that they could be forgiven for this rejection. Jesus is not the curse; Jesus is the cure!

The lostness of humankind is why the Church is seeking to evangelize the whole world. No alternate plan of salvation is known for those who do not hear the gospel. It would be unwise to speculate beyond what the Bible says on this matter. God himself determines what will happen to those who have not heard. God judges with perfect justice and never fails to do what is right. Importantly enough, you have heard the gospel, and you must respond to Jesus Christ. Jesus died on the cross to become the Saviour of the world, but He cannot become "your" Saviour until you receive Him.

FALSE FORMS OF CHRISTIANITY

The Bible forbids modifying any of its teachings or its Christ. Warnings are repeatedly given not to follow false gospels or false christs (Gal. 1:8; Matt. 24:24). Many who have been uncomfortable with accepting the teachings of Jesus at face value have opted to change Christianity to fit their own specifications. They have fashioned a Jesus in their own image and likeness. Truth for them becomes whatever they currently choose to believe. Their Jesus would never require them to evangelize, attend church, or oppose wrong viewpoints.

But what right do any of us have to change the

teachings of Christ? God has given Jesus all authority in heaven and earth (Matt.28:18). By what authority do we now correct Him? Nothing ever becomes true just because we believe it. To add or
subtract from Christianity leaves one with something other than the real thing. Those who teach
anything other than the true gospel are "accursed"
(Gal. 1:9). Jesus taught that the reason that the world
hates Him is because He exposed and condemned
the evil of this world (John 7:7). When the world
ceases to hate Jesus, it is always because it has
changed Him into someone He is not.

Christianity is God's way of salvation. Many
have rejected Jesus because they would rather find
their own way to God. Others have sought to modify
the teachings of Jesus to suit their own religious
preferences. Both decisions are rejections of Jesus
Christ. If Jesus really is the truth, then He is the
totality of truth for mankind. Christ must either be
accepted as is or rejected totally. There are many
false Christians who have changed the message of
Christianity. A true Christian is someone who follows Jesus Christ. Jesus said that He is the truth and
by trusting in Him the truth will make you free (John
8:32).

The problem with
Christianity is not that it has
been tried and found
wanting, but that it has been
found difficult, and
left untried.

G.K. Chesterton

6

INTELLECTUAL OBJECTIONS

Many times non-Christians enjoy posing objections to Christianity as reasons for not becoming Christians. Most of the time their objections are really not genuine questions but are excuses given as reasons not to believe. This chapter will examine the four most popular objections of skeptics about Christianity.

1. THE CHURCH IS FULL OF HYPOCRITES

One of the most frequently uttered charges leveled at Christianity is many non-Christians believe that the presence of hypocrites in the Church nullifies the entire structure of Christianity. However, the presence of hypocrites in the Church comes as no surprise to true Christians. Hypocrites have been alive and well in the Church for 2,000 years.

To dismiss Christianity on the basis of the presence of hypocrites displays a lack of understanding about the Christian Scriptures and the history of the Church. In responding to the charge that the Church is full of hypocrites, five truths concerning this matter should be considered.

First, God condemns hypocrisy.

The word hypocrite comes from the Greek word *hypokrites* which means "pretender or dissembler." It was originally used of Greek actors who uttered their lines behind masks. The word hypocrite was used to portray someone who was pretending to be someone else. A hypocrite is an actor, a person who pretends to be something but is not. Christ's harshest words were reserved for hypocrites:

> Woe to you, scribes and Pharisees, hypocrites! For you are like whitewashed tombs which appear beautifully outwardly, but inside are full of dead men's bones and all uncleanliness. Even so you also outwardly appear righteous to men, but inside you are full of hypocrisy and lawlessness (Matt. 23:27-28).

Jesus was abrupt with hypocrites because he knew the evil of hypocrisy. He knew how easily the charges of hypocrisy could discredit his work. The Scriptures repeatedly warn against hypocrisy (see 1 Tim. 4:1-2). Warnings are issued for true Christians to avoid association with them (1 Cor. 5:11). Jesus foretold the ultimate fate of hypocrites; they will be identified and separated from true Christians for judgment (see Matt. 7:21-23).

Second, there are some hypocrites in the Church.

The charge that the Church is "full" of hypocrites is certainly just not true. To even say that the majority of Christians are hypocrites is distantly removed from reality. The reality is that only a small minority of Christians in the Church are hypocrites. This is something that the Church has never denied. There have always been and will always be some hypocrites in the Church.

Throughout history the Church has worked hard to identify and remove hypocrites from its ranks. Such has been the case in recent days with the failings of a few prominent Christian leaders. But rather than congratulating the Church for its integrity, critics have focused on the negative.

Third, not all Christians are hypocrites.

It is wrong to condemn all Christians as hypocrites. Christians do not claim to be perfect. If Christianity claimed to be an organization for perfect people, then all Christians would be hypocrites.

Though not all Christians are hypocrites, all Christians are sinners. In fact, admitting that one is a sinner is a prerequisite to belonging to the Church. Public acknowledgment of one's sinful condition is a condition for membership. Though hypocrisy is a sin, being a sinner does not necessarily make someone guilty of hypocrisy. The terms "sinner" and "hypocrite" are not synonymous.

Many skeptics are actually guilty of imposing a double standard on Christians. They expect

Christians to hold to standards they themselves could never dream of attaining. Moreover, when Christians do try to live up to these standards, they are often accused of false piety and pretense.

Christians are not perfect; they are forgiven. They are seeking to become more Christ-like and godly in their conduct. The vast majority of Christians fall into this category. They are sincerely striving to live the Christian life.

Fourth, Christ is not a hypocrite.

When someone charges that the Church is full of hypocrites, they are really implying that because Christians fall short, Christianity also falls short. The central truth of Christianity does not rest in the performance of its followers but in the merit of its founder. Christianity stands or falls with the person of Jesus Christ.

Thus, the real question is not are there hypocrites in the Church, but rather, was Christ a hypocrite? If it can be proven that Christ was a hypocrite, then the whole structure of Christianity falls into ruins. The Scriptures present Jesus as nothing less than perfect. Jesus' disciples testified that Jesus was without sin (1 Pet. 2:22; 1 John 3:5). Christ himself challenged others to prove that He had ever sinned (John 8:46). The Scriptures present a perfect Christ for imperfect humans. Jesus was not a hypocrite. Therefore, to dismiss Christianity based on the existence of hypocrites is to dodge the real issue. It is illogical to reject Christianity for something that Christ himself denounced!

Last, the presence of hypocrites does not nullify the truthfulness of Christianity.

Many things of genuine value can be counter-feited whether it be money, art, or jewelry. The same is true of Christianity. Not all who claim to be Christians are genuine. However, the existence of the counterfeit does not negate the reality of the genuine.

Becoming a Christian is more than just joining the Church. In fact, becoming a member of a church does not guarantee that one is a Christian, nor does simply behaving in a religious way make one a Christian.

Not everyone who claims to be a Christian really is a true Christian. Thus, it is most illogical to dismiss true Christianity based on the existence of false Christianity. Concentrating on the worst of Christianity is no excuse for rejecting Christ. Becoming a true Christian is actually the opposite of being a hypocrite.

2. WHAT ABOUT THE ATROCITIES COMMITTED BY CHRISTIANS ?

Some contend that nothing good has ever come from Christianity. They charge Christianity with many horrible crimes including religious wars, the crusades, burning witches, the inquisition, and for some, the holocaust.

Before I answer these charges, it should be acknowledged that all of these charges assume Christian ethical standards of right and wrong. Why are acts such as murder and torture wrong? God forbids murder and torture. The standard by which the critic must judge Christianity is the ethical standards of the Scriptures.

Without a God, there would be no way to determine what is right or wrong. Without a universal standard, there is no method to discern evil or good. When man becomes his own standard of morality, morality becomes relative. This can quickly lead to moral anarchy. What exists as evil in one culture may be good in another. Who determines what is good or evil? Without a moral standard provided by God, there would be no universal standard of morality. What makes the slaughter of six million Jews in the holocaust wrong? The Germans believed that this was a necessary act that was not evil. By what standard can one say that so many people were wrong? Some have wrongly asserted that Hitler was a Christian. Though reared a Roman Catholic, Hitler rejected his upbringing and abandoned Christianity, which he considered to be the illegitimate offspring of Judaism. It also surprises some to learn that one-sixth of all the Jews killed by Hitler were professing Christians.

The issue of atrocities is simply an extension of the question of hypocrites. Much evil has been perpetrated by "so-called Christians" who did not practice true Christianity. Many so-called Christians who committed such acts were Christian in name only.

The Spanish Inquisition is such an example in that true Christians were the ones killed and tortured for their beliefs. Evangelical Christians were the victims and were not involved in the atrocities committed. Others have used the example of the crusades. However, the crusades must be put into the proper historical context.

The first crusade was generated by Muslims who captured Jerusalem and much of the Holy Land. Christians were slain, churches were burned, and all who did not convert were killed by the sword. Christians in Europe reacted by launching their own crusades to reclaim what was previously lost. Many terrible atrocities occurred as happens in all wars. When one considers that the so-called Christian crusades were responses to the Muslim war, then balance and perspective are found.

Others have mistakenly charged that more people have died in religious wars than all the other wars put together. Actually the atheistic systems of Nazi Germany and Soviet Marxism are responsible for many million more deaths of people than the number of people wrongly slain in the name of Christianity. In fact, in the last 50 years, more than 150 million people have been killed by atheistic governments.[1] Adolf Hitler was responsible for between 11 and 16 million deaths. Joseph Stalin was responsible for killing 40 million. Mao Tse-tung is estimated to be responsible for 72 million deaths. More people have been killed by 20th century atheist states than in all the other wars combined in history.

Focusing on the atrocities of so-called Christians for some is really a smoke screen to avoid the real issue. Christianity has far more positive achievements than negative influences. Christianity has been instrumental in the formation of countless hospitals, schools, colleges, orphanages, relief agencies, and charity agencies. No other organization in history can compare to achievements of the Christian Church.

3. CHRISTIANITY IS A CRUTCH
FOR THE WEAK

Karl Marx said that "Religion is the opiate of the masses." Critics such as Marx have charged that religion is simply invented by humans. Religion is an invention designed for people who are incapable of coping with the pressures of life. To these weaker people, religion is an emotional crutch. Such critics assume that Christianity is subjective primarily because it provides emotional comfort. Some respond that they do not feel a need for this type of emotional comfort as though that fact falsifies Christianity. Such individuals often claim to be "stronger" because they are brave enough to face life without a crutch. Because they are not addicted to religion, they are free to live outside of the repressive rules of religion.

INVENTING GOD

The difficult question secular philosophy has had to answer is, "If there is no God, why are so many people religious?" Scholars of the 19th century set out to answer this question by launching a discipline called "comparative religious studies." Many involved in this academic discipline conclude that religion is simply the product of evolution.

Many scholars influenced by Darwin's theory of evolution applied the same evolutionary principles to religion. English scholar Sir Edward Burnett Tylor popularized this view in his work *Primitive Cultures*, published in 1871. Tylor and others held that religion evolved from animism to polytheism and finally to monotheism. Monotheism was presumed to be the most advanced form of worship as one of the polytheistic gods was exalted above the others.

This theory has been discredited in light of evidence proving otherwise. Even the oldest cultures give evidence of religious traditions, many of which held the belief of supreme God. This trait is found in many animistic religions. Instead of religion evolving into monotheism, it rather appears that monotheism de-evolved into animism and polytheism.

Sigmund Freud contended that man invented God in order to tame nature. The only way to tame the forces of impersonal nature would be to make them personal. Thus, man creates the ultimate crutch — a personal God.

The problem with the theories of Freud, Marx, Satre, Russell, and others who have charged that Christianity is a crutch, is they begin with a false premise. They all assume that there is no God but provide no evidence for this falsification.

The question of the origin of religions is not psychological but historical. There is a vast difference in how religion could have started and how it actually began. It seems quite doubtful that someone with a fear problem would invent the God of the Bible. One would be far more likely to invent a less threatening god who could be more easily managed or appeased.

ATHEISM IS A CRUTCH

In a very real sense, it must be acknowledged that the God of the Scriptures is a threat. In fact, the biblical God can be much more frightening than the forces found in nature. Much about this God can evoke feelings of terror. His attributes of being holy, all-powerful, all-knowing, and unchanging can be quite disturbing to humans.

By eliminating God, the atheist alleviates the fear of having to face such a being in the judgment. If one could rid oneself of this kind of God, much guilt could be alleviated. Thus, could not the case be made that atheism is a crutch — a crutch which alleviates the fear of facing God?

WHAT IS YOUR CRUTCH?

To imply that non-religious people do not need crutches is misleading. Crutches such as drugs, alcohol, sexual addiction, cigarettes, money, power, and material possessions demonstrate that religion is not the only crutch. Atheism can become a crutch for those addicted to a lifestyle contrary to God's standards of morality.

It is a false assumption that just because one is a Christian, one is weak. Christians are not weak. Christians face difficulty daily as they strive to follow God. Christians endure rejection, ridicule, and persecution for their beliefs. It would be a much easier path not to stand for Christ. Those who believe Christians are weak do not fully appreciate the difficulty of the Christian life.

Everyone needs a crutch. The question is, what will we lean upon for support? Christianity provides what atheism never can.

First, Christianity provides spiritual fulfillment.

Man needs and depends upon God. True fulfillment can only be found in God. Just as cars depend upon gas, so man depends upon God. Man cannot live by bread alone (material things) but craves spiritual fulfillment (Matt. 4:4).

Second, Christianity provides peace.

Peace is the quest of every human being. If it could be sold, people would pay any price. Christ alone gives peace (Matt. 11:28). He gives a peace that passes understanding. Ephesians 2:14 says that Christ himself is our peace.

Lastly, Christianity provides forgiveness.

Christianity provides the solution to the problem of guilt. The critic may respond that it is religion itself that is the source of guilt, and guilt is only a religious problem. But is that true? Not to have any guilt feeling would be most abnormal. Sociopaths who kill without remorse are considered sick and abnormal. Guilt is not an abnormal feeling.

Christianity does not offer a "crutch" for the guilt problem, it offers a "cure." The Scriptures teach that Christ died for our sins so that forgiveness could become a reality. Normal people feel guilt. Christianity is not just for weak people; it is for normal people as well.

4. WHY THERE IS EVIL AND SUFFERING

One of the strongest challenges of the Christian faith comes in the problem of human suffering. This topic is commonly referred to by theologians and philosophers as "the problem of evil."

While the Christian points to the various evidences found in the universe that cannot be explained without a God, the skeptic points to other phenomena which are alleged to be inconsistent with the existence of God. The problem of evil has been called the "Achilles heel" of Christianity.

Epicurus, who lived 300 years before Christ, laid out this classical argument which is as follows:

1. God is all powerful (omniscient)
2. God is good (omnibenevolent)
3. Evil and suffering exist.

Many skeptics have charged that this is inconsistent. They say that all three cannot be true at the same time. Skeptic David Hume wrote, "Epicurus' old questions are yet unanswered. Is he willing to prevent evil, but not able? then he is impotent. Is he able, but not willing? then he is malevolent. Is he both able and willing? whence then is evil?"[2]

The thrust of the charge is that the presence of evil disproves the existence of God. But is the presence of evil really inconsistent with the God of the Scriptures? In the following five points, I will provide a theodicy (a defense of God's goodness and power in light of the problem of evil) which shows otherwise.

First, God did not originate evil.

The world was not created in the evil state that it is today. The first chapter of Genesis depicts a world free from sin and suffering. Sin entered the world through Adam's disobedience. Through sin, evil was brought into the world. This rebellion is referred to as the fall of man. Man became separated from God. Because of the Fall, the world is in an abnormal state. Nature and the animal kingdom can be hostile toward man as a result of the Fall (Gen. 3:17-19). Even between fellow humans, man engages in continual conflict since the Fall.

Adam was the corporate head of all humans. The name *Adam* in the Hebrew language means mankind. When Adam sinned, he represented the entire human race, acting as any other person would have in the same position. Just as Adam, we also have rebelled against God and are guilty and deserving of justice (Rom. 3:23).

Many object to being punished for something that Adam did. But this complaint does not reflect the fact that we are guilty enough of our own sins. The key is realizing that God is not responsible for sin, people are. Evil is actually not a thing but a corruption of a good thing. God's creation was originally pronounced as good by God himself (Gen 1:31). However, man corrupted the creation by not following the instructions given for the perfect creation.

Though God did not create evil, He did create a world in which evil is possible. There is a vital reason why.

Evil is necessary for a free world.

Though God made evil "possible," the rebellion of humankind made evil "actual." Evil is a necessity in a free world. Free choice gives possibility to wrong choice. Evil is a necessary part of free will.

The result of Adam's poor decision shattered the good creation like the effects of an atomic bomb. Evil is not discretionary; like a bomb, the innocent may be injured by the blast. With wrong choices come severe consequences. For choices to be meaningful, there must be consequences. Imagine trying to discipline a young child without being able to enforce consequences for bad behavior. Thus, if God did not punish sin, sin would not preserve its moral character. This also means that in a world where evil is allowed to thrive, innocent suffering will occur. In order to provide full moral freedom, it is evident that God must allow innocent suffering. This begs the question, "Why couldn't God make a world without any evil?" The answer lies in what it means to be free. Could God have created free creatures that could not sin?

God could have created humans to be like robots, controlling our every move. He could have designed humans to behave exactly as programmed. But how would you like to be married to a mechanical doll? You could program it to love you by simply pulling a string to which it would mouth the words "I love you."

But would the mechanical doll "really" love you, or would it simply do what you programmed it to do? True love is voluntary. It is also risky. Just as courage is only possible where there is true danger; love is only possible where there is true freedom. Though in this imperfect world, the innocent do suffer, God thought it worth the risk to allow freedom. Whereas this is not the best world, it is the best way to the best world.

Third, there is an important reason God hesitates to stop evil.

The skeptic charges that if God is omnipotent and omnibenevolent, why is there evil? Some have challenged that God may either not be omnipotent or not omnibenevolent. The theological assumption of skeptics concerning the argument surrounding God's omnipotence and omnibenevolence has a flawed assumption. The assumption is that a good being will always eliminate all the suffering it is possible to prevent. They ignore the fact that God might have important reasons for allowing evil.

Just as parents often allow their children to make mistakes and suffer, God similarly acts in a parental fashion with His creation. God allows suffering and evil to achieve a higher goal. In truth, God cannot destroy evil without destroying freedom. God's ultimate purpose is that evil be defeated, not simply destroyed.

We must realize that God is in the process of solving a cosmic revolution. The revolution began with Satan who introduced cosmic evil. Then human evil entered the scene through Adam.

What if God simply "zapped" people out of existence every time they revolted? Would not this confirm that He was not truly omnibenevolent? And how many people would God have to zap before the world could be safe and evil be eradicated for good? Simply "zapping" a large number of rebels would not solve the problem of evil. If you do not believe me, read the story of Noah in the Book of Genesis. God destroyed the evil but left potential evil behind in the survivors.

An important point to grasp in understanding the problem of evil is understanding that God is not interested in the partial containment of evil. This is what most skeptics are referring to when they ask,

158 • REASONS FOR BELIEVING

"What is God doing about suffering?" What the skeptic is really challenging is the process of the eradication of evil. Often, arrogant assumptions are made by those who challenge that God is not presently dealing with the problem of evil. Hypocritically, many skeptics who object to suffering do not lift a finger to feed the hungry or clothe the naked.

The cause of Christ is to alleviate the suffering of this world. It is hard to understand criticism of the one being in the universe committed to good. Is it not profoundly evil to reject that which is inherently good?

The skeptic implies that because God has not done anything today, He never will. What if God did step in each day and prevent all evil acts? He could begin by stopping all rapes, all murders, all crimes. But how much evil should God stop each day to be considered good? What if He stopped all sin altogether? Most people would object because their freedoms would be gone. The skeptic wants to tell God how He can handle the eradication process. Humankind wants a safe, sterile playground for its sin — free from the interference of God, but backed by His protection for the wrong choices of others.

Instead of partially stopping evil, God has chosen to let the revolution fully develop. Rather than an endless series of revolts and eradications, God will put an end to the revolt with the return of Jesus Christ. The day God steps in to stop evil will mean the cessation of the opportunity to trust Christ. God desires that as many as possible attain salvation and delays His coming for that very reason (2 Pet. 3:9).

Not all suffering is bad.

Many hold that pain is evidence against God's existence. However, pain can be used for good and bad purposes. Not all pain is evil. Pain is an essential mechanism for survival. Without pain, the body is stripped of vital protection. The initial pain of touching a hot stove can help a child to avoid permanent damage to his/her hand. Pain is an important signal to warn of even greater danger. Body pain can often lead to a medical visit which can provide early treatment to potentially devastating medical conditions.

Suffering is a signal. It can also be a spiritual signal which reminds us of the fragile balance of life and of our own morality. C. S. Lewis, in his well-known book *The Problem of Pain*, notes that suffering "removes the veil; it plants the flag of truth within the fortress of a rebel soul."[3] Lewis writes, "God whispers to us in our pleasure, speaks to us in our conscience, but shouts to us in our pains; it is his megaphone to rouse a deaf world."[4]

Some suffering and evil actually helps to bring greater good. This is best seen in the suffering of Christ. On the Cross, God took His own medicine. God has traveled down the road of pain, suffering, loneliness, and death — a road which led to the Cross. Skeptics who point to the problem of pain must understand that God himself suffered. He has felt the pain of men. Christ is not just a Saviour, he is our suffering Saviour.

The Cross is the ultimate example of the innocent suffering. The question is, "Why would God allow his own son to die when he had done nothing wrong?" The higher purpose of the Cross is seen in the fact that Christ served as our substitute and paid the penalty for our sins. The Cross is not seen as defeat but as victory. God used Christ's suffering to defeat evil. Christ's suffering was not pointless. The resurrection of Christ demonstrates that the sufferings of Christ assure His followers of eternal glory. This is the hope of the Christian.

Becoming a Christian does not mean that one will be free from suffering. The Christian understands that the sufferings of this life are outweighed by the glory that is to come in the next life (Rom. 8:18). Suffering and glorification are part of the same process in the Christian life (Rom. 8:14-18). The hope of heaven enables the Christian to cope with suffering in a way those without hope will never experience. The Christian looks to the day that all suffering will be gone:

> And God will wipe away every tear from their eyes; there shall be no more death, nor sorrow, nor crying. There shall be no more pain, for the former things have passed away (Rev. 21:4).

Many critics of Christianity have charged that suffering is just not fair. Many blame God for all the suffering that takes place as though God is the cause of all suffering. This view would actually be more accurate of Hinduism's concept of the law of Karma which teaches that all suffering is the result of previous evil-doing.

The Scriptures teach that not all suffering is related to wrongdoing. Jesus corrected the Pharisees and His disciples of thinking wrongly that misfortune was due to personal sin (see John 9:1-3). This type of wrong theology has been used by many skeptics to reject Christianity on false grounds.

Jesus responded to such an accusation in Luke 13. Jesus was questioned about the deaths of 18 people who were killed by the collapse of the tower of Siloam. The question takes the form of, "Why did God allow all these innocent people to die?" Jesus' answer was astonishing, "Unless you repent you will all likewise perish." Jesus' answer reveals the fact that the wrong question was being asked. He did not allow the question to become a smoke screen for dealing with the real issue at hand.

At the heart of the issue is the underlying challenge that God is not fair. The problem lies in the fact that society holds pleasure as its chief goal in life. This philosophy is known as *hedonism*. To those who live by this philosophy, suffering in any form is found to be very offensive. To say that God is not fair is a very dangerous charge.

If God gave us what we deserved, we would be in big trouble. It would be foolish to ask God for justice; what we need is mercy. If we received justice, all of us would be destroyed. God's mercy and grace are so taken for granted that we are shocked by suffering and pain.

One wonders why no one ever asks why we do not suffer more than we presently do. Instead of wondering why the tower fell on the 18 people, they should have been asking why the tower did not fall on them. Instead of questioning God's justice, perhaps we need to give Him thanks for His mercy.

Last, God has a solution to the problem of evil.

God hates evil. God has defeated evil and the day will soon come when evil will cease. Evil and suffering are temporary; all pain will one day be eliminated. Though evil is very real, it is also very temporary.

The day God deals with evil, he will deal with all evil. This is the promise of the coming perfect world. In the meantime, God is striving for as many as possible to be saved. The sad fact is that many will make the decision not to be a part of God's heaven. God will not send them to hell, they will send themselves. For God to force people to go to heaven against their wishes would not be heaven — it would be hell. Atheist Jean-Paul Sarte noted that the gates of hell are locked from the inside by the free choice of men.

Hell will be a place which features the worst possible suffering imaginable. No suffering on earth can compare to this horrible place. All who reject Christ will be cast into the lake of fire (Rev. 20:15). As horrible as this place is, you do not have to go there; it is your decision. The very fact that evil exists is so that you can make this choice. How will you decide?

And if anyone hears My words
and does not believe, I do not
judge him; for I did not come
to judge the world but to save
the world. He who rejects Me,
and does not receive My words,
has that which judges him —
the word that I have spoken
will judge him in the last day.

Jesus Christ
Son of God

John 12:47-48

7

CONCLUSION — THE VERDICT

When you first began reading this book, perhaps you put God on trial to see if He is real. But as you read, you quickly discovered that the true defendant on trial is you. But please do not get the wrong idea that God is purposely trying to condemn you. God is not out to get you. Jesus did not come to be your "judge"—he came to be your "Saviour."

Neither this book nor Christianity's purpose is to make you feel guilty. You already feel guilty because you are guilty. Christianity is the solution to your problem. So often people act like Christianity is a big imposition with which they do not want to be bothered. They do not want their lives to be complicated by "the God problem." But in truth, salvation is God's solution to man's problem.

MAN'S PROBLEM

Man's fundamental problem is sin. Romans 3:23 says, "For all have sinned and come short of the glory of God." Sin is rebellion against God. Man was created for eternal fellowship with God but broke this fellowship through disobedience. Because of this, we are separated from God. Romans 6:23 states, "For the wages of sin is death." Sin cannot be accepted by the Holy God (Rev. 21:27).

Sin first brings physical death and is the ultimate cause of spiritual death which is eternal separation from God. Spiritual death occurs when man dies in his sin (John 8:24). Man is not merely out of fellowship with God; he is dead to God (Eph. 2:1). What can a dead person do? Nothing! Man cannot save himself. Acts 4:12 says, "Nor is there salvation in any other, for there is no other name [Jesus] under heaven given among men, by which we must be saved."

Man cannot earn salvation by good works (Eph. 2:8). We are already condemned and have been judged as unrighteous by God (John 3:17-18).

GOD'S SOLUTION

God requires man to repent of his sin. Second Peter 3:9 states, "The Lord . . . is longsuffering toward us, not willing that any should perish but that all should come to repentance." Repentance means to change your life's direction. It involves turning away from your present road of rebellion against God and going down the road which leads to Jesus Christ. Repentance is not just being sorry for your sins, repentance is a decision to change allegiance from sin and self to follow Jesus Christ as Lord and Saviour.

True repentance leads to receiving Christ by faith. John 1:12 says, "But as many as received him, to them he gave the right to become children of God." Becoming a Christian is more than just believing facts about Jesus, it is about personally accepting what Christ has done for you. Mere intellectual belief in God will not get you into heaven (James 2:19). You must commit your life to Christ to follow Him as your personal Lord and Saviour. Trusting Jesus means that He becomes your king. If you are not willing to live the Christian life then you cannot become a Christian. Jesus' call is to follow Him (Mark 2:14). That is what a Christian is: a follower of Jesus Christ. You can receive Christ by prayer. The Bible says, "For whoever calls upon the name of the Lord shall be saved" (Rom. 10:13).

This decision is the most important decision you will ever make. Do not delay — make your decision as soon as possible. Do not make the mistake of thinking that all doubts must be removed before trusting Christ. You must be willing to trust Christ for what He has done for you in the past, and leave the future to Him. I suggest you pray something like this:

Dear God;
I now confess to You that I am a sinner.

*As best I know how, I will turn from my sin
and place my trust in You. I believe that
You died for me on the cross and rose again
from the grave. I ask that You forgive me of
my sin as I now receive Your gift of eternal
life. In Jesus name. Amen.*

A CHANGED LIFE

When you receive Jesus into your heart, He will
change your life. Second Corinthians 5:17 states,
"Therefore if anyone is in Christ, he is a new
creation; old things have passed away; behold, all
things have become new." The Holy Spirit will give
you internal confirmation that you are a child of God
(Rom. 8:16). The Bible refers to your conversion as
a new birth (John 3:3). You are made new in the
Spirit and placed into the body of Christ. The way
that you can know this has occurred is through the
internal witness of the Holy Spirit and the outward
evidence of a changed life (James 2:17). A changed
life is the most powerful evidence that a person is a
Christian. The lack of a changed life is likewise a
strong indicator of the absence of Jesus Christ in a
person's life.

When you receive Christ, the first step that you
will want to take is to publicly profess Jesus Christ
in a local fellowship of believers. Be sure and find
a church which teaches salvation through faith,
believes in the authority of the Bible, and demonstrates a love for reaching others in evangelism. As
you serve Christ in your local church, pray, read
your Bible, and share your faith with others. Please

take the truths of this book and share them with a hurting world which longs to hear the truth about Jesus Christ.

ENDNOTES

Chapter One

[1]Colin Brown, *Philosophy and the Christian Faith* (Wheaton, IL: Tyndale, 1971), p. 147.

[2]Robert E. D. Clark, *Darwin: Before and After* (London: Paternoster, 1950), p. 86.

[3]Henry Morris, *The Bible and Modern Science* (Chicago, IL: Moody Press, 1951), p. 34.

[4]Lewis Carroll, *Through the Looking-Glass* and *What Alice Found There,* in *The Complete Illustrated Words of Lewis Carroll,* ed. Edward Guiliano (New York, NY: Avenell Books, 1982), p. 127-28.

[5]Paul S. Taylor, *The Illustrated Origins Answer Book* (Mesa, AZ: Eden Publications, 1993), p. 8.

[6]Cora A. Reno, *Evolution on Trial* (Chicago, IL: Moody Press, 1970), p. 103.

[7]Walter T. Brown, Jr., *In the Beginning* (Phoenix, AZ: Center for Scientific Creation, 1989), p. 2.

[8]Taylor, *The Illustrated Origins Answer Book,* p. 25.

[9]Michael Denton, *Evolution: A Theory in Crisis* (Bethesda, MD: Adler & Adler, 1986), p. 330-31.

[10]John C. Whitcomb, *The Early Earth* (Grand Rapids, MI: Baker Book House, 1986), p. 103.

[11]F. Hitching, *The Neck of the Giraffe: Where Darwin Went Wrong* (New Haven, CT: Ticknor & Fields, 1982), p. 85-6.

[12]Scott M. Huse, *The Collapse of Evolution* (Grand Rapids, MI: Baker Books, 1993), p. 92.

[13]Richard B. Bliss, Gary E. Parker, Duane T. Gish, *In Search of the Origin of Life* (San Diego, CA: C.L.P. Publishers, 1979), p. 35.

[14]Henry M. Morris, *The Biblical Basis for Modern Science* (Grand Rapids, MI: Baker Book House, 1984), p. 232.

[15]Taylor, *The Illustrated Origins Answer Book,* p. 9.

[16]Huse, *The Collapse of Evolution,* p. 117.

[17]Ibid.

[18]Ibid.

[19]Bird, p. 72.
[20]Brown, *In the Beginning,* p. iii.
[21]Ibid.
[22]Norman Geisler and Ron Brooks, *When Skeptics Ask* (Wheaton, IL: Victor Books, 1990), p.22.
[23]Carl Sagan, F. H. C. Crick, L. M. Muchin; Carl Sagan, ed., *Communication with Extraterrestrial Intelligence* (Cambridge, MA: MIT Press), p. 45-46.
[24]Brown, *In the Beginning,* p. 7.
[25]Sir Fred Hoyle, "Hoyle on Evolution," *Nature,* vol. 294 (Nov. 12, 1981), p. 105.
[26]Huse, *The Collapse of Evolution,* p. 59.
[27]Morris, *The Biblical Basis for Modern Science,* p. 150.
[28]Brown, *In the Beginning,* p. 11.
[29]Ibid.
[30]Ross, p. 128.
[31]D. D. Riegle, *Creation or Evolution* (Grand Rapids, MI: Zondervan Publishing House, 1971), p. 18.
[32]Ibid.
[33]Huse, *The Collapse of Evolution,* p. 72.
[34]Riegle, *Creation or Evolution* , p. 18-19.
[35]Morris, *The Biblical Basis for Modern Science,* p. 156.
[36]Robert Jastrow, *God and the Astronomers* (New York, NY: W.W. Norton & Co., 1978), p. 15.
[37]Norman L. Geisler, *Philosophy of Religion* (Grand Rapids, MI: Zondervan, 1974), p. 190-226.

Chapter Two
[1]Adapted from Josh McDowell, *Evidence That Demands a Verdict*, rev. ed. (San Bernardino, CA: Here's Life, 1979), p. 42.
[2]Source unknown.

Chapter Three
[1]Peter W. Stoner, *Science Speaks* (Chicago, IL: Moody Press, 1969), p. 109.
[2]Ignatius, Ephesians, p. 18.2-19.1.

Chapter Four

[1]Thomas Arnold, *Christian Life — Its Hopes, Its Fears, and Its Close* (London: T. Fellowes, 1859, 6th ed.), p. 324.

[2]Quoted in Michael Green, *Man Alive* (Downers Grove, IL: InterVarsity Press, 1968), p. 54.

[3]Gaston Foote, *The Transformation of the Twelve* (Nashville, TN: Abingdon Press, 1958), p. 12.

[4]C. F. D. Moule, *The Phenomenon of the New Testament* (London: SCM, 1967), p. 3.

[5]T. Peters, *CBQ* 35 [1973], p. 481.

[6]Josephus, *Ant.* iv. 8.15 [219].

Chapter 6

[1]Robert A. Morey, *The New Atheism and the Erosion of Freedom* (Minn., MN: Bethany, 1986), p. 148-49.

[2]David Hume, *Dialogues Concerning Natural Religion*, ed. Norman Kemp Smith (New York, NY: Thomas Nelson & Sons, 1947; Library of Liberal Arts, 1979), p. 198.

[3]C. S. Lewis, *The Problem of Pain* (London: Geoffrey Bles, 1940), p. 83.

[4]Ibid., p. 81.

Bibliography

Adams, Robert. "Moral Arguments for Theistic Belief." In *Rationality and Religious Belief*, ed. by C. F. Delaney, p. 116-40. Notre Dame, IN: University of Notre Dame Press, 1979.

Adler, Mortimer J. *Ten Philosophical Mistakes*. New York, NY: Collier, 1985.

_____ *Truth in Religion: The Plurality of Religions and the Unity of Truth*. New York, NY: MacMillan, 1990.

Adler, Mortimer, and Charles Van Doren. *How to Read a Book*. New York, NY: Touchstone, 1972.

Anderson, Charles. *The Historical Jesus: A Continuing Quest*. Grand Rapids, MI: Eerdmans, 1972.

Anderson, J. N. D. *Christianity and Comparative Religion*. London: Tyndale Press, 1970.

_____ *Christianity: The Witness of History*. Downers Grove, IL: InterVarsity Press, 1970.

_____ *A Lawyer Among the Theologians*. Grand Rapids, MI: Eerdmans, 1974.

Anderson, Norman. *Christianity and World Religions*. 2d ed. Downers Grove, IL: InterVarsity, 1984.

Ankerberg, John, and John Weldon. *Encyclopedia of New Age Beliefs*. Eugene, OR: Harvest House, 1996.

Aquinas, Thomas. *Summa Contra Gentiles*, in *Basic Writings of Saint Thomas Aquinas*. Edited by Anton Pegis. New York, NY: Random House, 1945.

_____ *Summa Theologica*, in *Great Books of the Western World*. Vols. 28-29. Edited by Robert Maynard Hutchins. Chicago, IL: Encyclopedia Britannica, 1952.

Barnett, Paul. *Is the New Testament Reliable?* Downers Grove, IL: InterVarsity Press, 1986.

Beisner, E. Calvin. *Answers for Atheists, Agnostics, and Other Thoughtful Skeptics: Dialogues About Christian Faith and Life*. Rev. ed. Wheaton, IL: Crossway Books, 1993.

Blocher, Henri. *In the Beginning: The Opening Chapters of Genesis*. trans. by David G. Preston. Downers Grove, IL: InterVarsity Press, 1984.

Blomberg, Craig L. *The Historical Reliability of the Gospels*. Downers Grove, IL: InterVarsity Press, 1987.

Boa, Kenneth. *God, I Don't Understand*. Wheaton, IL: Victor Books, 1975.

_____ *Cults, World Religions, and You*. Wheaton, IL: Victor Books, 1977.

Boice, James Montgomery. *Does Inerrancy Matter?* Oakland, CA: International Council on Biblical Inerrancy, 1979.

_____ ed. *The Foundation of Biblical Authority*. Grand Rapids, MI: Zondervan, 1978.

Brown, Colin, ed. *History, Criticism & Faith*. Downers Grove, IL: InterVarsity Press, 1976.

_____ *Miracles and the Critical Mind*. Grand Rapids, MI: Eerdmans, 1984.

Bruce, F. F. *The New Testament Documents: Are They Reliable?* Downers Grove, IL: InterVarsity Press.

Carnell, Edward J. *An Introduction to Christian Apologetics*. Grand Rapids, MI: Eerdmans, 1950.

_____ *A Philosophy of the Christian Religion*. Grand Rapids, MI: Eerdmans, 1952.

_____ *The Case for Biblical Christianity*. Ed. by Roland H. Nash. Grand Rapids, MI: Eerdmans, 1969.

Casserly, J. V. Langmead. *Apologetics and Evangelism*. Philadelphia, PA: Westminster, 1962.

Chesterton, G. K. *Orthodoxy*. Garden City, NY: Image/Doubleday, 1959.

Clark, Robert E. D. *Science and Christianity — A Partnership*. Mountain View, CA: Pacific Press, 1972.

Coppedge, James F. *Evolution: Possible or Impossible?* Grand Rapids, MI: Zondervan, 1973.

Craig, William Lane. *The Existence of God and the Beginning of the Universe*. San Bernardino, CA: Here's Life Pub., 1979.

_____ *The Kalam Cosmological Argument*. New York, NY: MacMillan, 1979.

_____ *The Son Rises: Historical Evidence for the Resurrection of Jesus Christ*. Chicago, IL: Moody, 1982.

Davidheiser, Bolton. *Evolution and Christian Faith*. Philadelphia, PA: Presbyterian & Reformed, 1969.

Davies, Brian. *An Introduction to the Philosophy of Religion*. Oxford: Oxford University Press, 1982.

DeWitt, David A. *Answering the Tough Ones*. Chicago, IL: Moody, 1980.

Ewing, A. C. *Value and Reality*. London: George Allen & Unwin, 1973.

Ferando, Ajith. *The Supremacy of Christ*. Wheaton, IL: Crossway, 1995.

Frair, Wayne, and Percival Davis. *A Case for Creation*. 3d ed. Chicago, IL: Moody, 1983.

France, R. T. *The Evidence for Jesus*. Downers Grove, IL: InterVarsity Press, 1986.

Geisler, Norman L. *Christ: The Theme of the Bible*. Chicago, IL: Moody, 1969.

_____ *Christian Apologetics*. Grand Rapids, MI: Baker, 1976.

_____ *Miracles and Modern Thought*. Grand Rapids, MI: Zondervan, 1982.

_____ ed. *Inerrancy*. Gand Rapids, MI: Zondervan, 1980.

_____ *When Skeptics Ask: A Handbook of Christian Evidences*. Wheaton, IL: Victor Books, 1990.

Geisler, Norman L., and Ronald M. Brooks. *Come, Let Us Reason: An Introduction to Logical Thinking*. Grand Rapids, MI: 1990.

Geisler, Norman L., and William Watkins. *Perspectives: Understanding and Evaluating Today's World Views*. San Bernardino, CA: Here's Life Pub., 1984.

Geivett, Douglas. *Evil and the Evidence for God*. Philadelphia, PA: Temple University Press, 1993.

Geivett, Douglas, and Gary Habermas, eds. *Miracles: Has God Acted in History?* Downers Grove, IL: InterVarsity, 1997.

Gerstner, John. *Reasons for Faith*. Grand Rapids, MI: Baker Book House, 1967.

Gill, Jerry H. *The Possibility of Religious Knowledge*. Grand Rapids, MI: Eerdmans, 1971.

Green, Michael. *Man Alive!* Chicago, IL: InterVarsity Press, 1967.

_____ *Evangelism in the Early Church*. Grand Rapids, MI: Eerdmans, 1970.

Guiness, Os. *The Dust of Death*. Downers Grove, IL: InterVarsity Press, 1973.

_____ *God in the Dark: the Assurance of Faith Beyond a Shadow of Doubt*. Wheaton, IL: Crossway, 1996.

Gutteridge, Don J., Jr. *The Defense Rests Its Case*. Nashville, TN: Broadman Press, 1975.

Habermas, Gary R. *The Resurrection of Jesus: An Apologetic*. Grand Rapids, MI: Baker Book House, 1980.

Habermas, Gary R., and Anthony . N. Flew. *Did Jesus Rise from the Dead?* Terry L. Miethe, ed. San Francisco, CA: Harper & Row, 1987.

Hackett, Stuart C. *The Reconstruction of the Christian Revelation Claim: A Philosophical and Critical Apologetic*. Grand Rapids, MI: Baker, 1984.

Ham, Ken. *The Lie: Evolution*. Green Forest, AR: Master Books, 1987.

Hanna, Mark M. *Crucial Questions in Apologetics*. Grand Rapids, MI: Baker, 1981.

Harris, R. Laird. *Inspiration and Canonicity of the Bible*. Grand Rapids, MI: Zondervan, 1957.

Hitching, Francis. *The Neck of the Giraffe: Where Darwin Went Wrong*. New Haven, CT: Ticknor & Fields, 1982.

Holmes, Arthur F. *Faith Seeks Understanding*. Grand Rapids, MI: Eerdmans, 1971.

Hoover, A. J. *Don't You Believe It*. Chicago, IL: Moody Press.

Hoyle, Fred, and Chandra Wickramasinghe. *Evolution from Space*. London: J. M. Dent, 1981.

Hume, David. *Dialogues Concerning Natural Religion*, ed. Norman Kemp Smith. New York, NY: Nelson, 1947; Library of Liberal Arts, 1979.

Jaki, Stanley. *God and the Cosmologists*. Washington D.C.: Regnery Gateway, 1989.

Jastrow, Robert. *God and the Astronomers*. New York, NY: W. W. Norton, 1978.

Johnson, David L. *A Reasoned Look at Asian Religions*. Minneapolis, MN: Bethany, 1985.

Johnson, Phillip E. *Darwin on Trial*. Washington, D.C.: Regnery Gateway, 1991.

____ *Reason in the Balance: The Case Against Naturalism in Science, Law, and Education*. Downers Grove, IL: InterVarsity Press, 1995.

Kennedy, D. James, and Jerry Newcomb. *What If Jesus Had Never Been Born?* Nashville, TN: Nelson, 1994.

Kreeft, Peter. *Between Heaven and Hell*. Downers Grove, IL: InterVarsity Press, 1982.

Kreeft, Peter, and Ronald Tacelli. *Handbook of Christian Apologetics*. Downers Grove, IL: InterVarsity Press, 1994.

Ladd, George E. *I Believe in the Resurrection of Jesus*. Grand Rapids, MI: Eerdmans, 1975.

Lewis, C. S. *The Abolition of Man*. New York, NY: MacMillan, 1947.

____ *Miracles, A Preliminary Study*. New York, NY: MacMillan, 1947.

____ *Mere Christianity*. New York, NY: MacMillan, 1952.

____ *The Problem of Pain*. New York, NY: MacMillan, 1962.

____ *God in the Dock*. Edited by Walter Hooper. Grand Rapids, MI: Eerdmans, 1970.

Lewis, Gordon R. *Decide for Yourself: A Theological Workbook* (1970) and *Think for Yourself*. Downers Grove, IL: InterVarsity Press.

____ *Judge for Yourself*. Downers Grove, IL: InterVarsity Press, 1974.

____ *Testing Christianity's Truth Claims*. Chicago, IL: Moody, 1976.

Linneman, Eta. *Historical Criticism of the Bible: Methodology or Ideology?* Grand Rapids, MI: Baker, 1990.

Linton, Irwin H. *A Lawyer Examines the Bible*. Grand Rapids, MI: Baker, 1943.

Little, Paul E. *Know Why You Believe*. Wheaton, IL: Victor Books, 1968.

Locke, John. *The Reasonableness of Christianity*. Edited by I. T. Ramsey. Stanford, CA: Stanford U. Press, 1958.

Mangalwadi, Vishal. *The World of Gurus*. Rev. ed. New Delhi: Vikas Pub., 1987.

Marshall, I. Howard. *Luke: Historian and Theologian*. Grand Rapids, MI: Zondervan, 1971.

____ *I Believe in the Historical Jesus*. Grand Rapids, MI: Eerdmans, 1977.

Martin, Walter. *The Kingdom of the Cults*. Rev. ed. Minneapolis: Bethany.

____ *The New Cults*. Santa Ana, CA: Vision House.

Martyr, Justin. *First Apology in Early Christian Fathers*. ed. by Cyril C. Richardson. Philadelphia, PA: Westminster, 1953.

____ *Second Apology*, in *The Ante-Nicene Fathers*. Vol. 1. Edited by Alexander Roberts and James Donaldson. Grand Rapids, MI: Eerdmans, 1975.

____ *Dialogue with Trypho*, in *The Ante-Nicene Fathers*. Vol. 1. Edited by Alexander Roberts and James Donaldson. Grand Rapids, MI: Eerdmans, 1975.

McCallum, Dennis, gen. ed. *The Death of Truth: What's Wrong with Multi-Culturalism, the Rejection of Reason and the New Post-Modern Diversity?* Minneapolis, MN: Bethany, 1996.

McDowell, Josh. *Evidence That Demands a Verdict*. Vols. 1 and 2. San Bernardino, CA: Campus Crusade for Christ, 1972, 1975.

____ *More Than a Carpenter*. Wheaton, IL: Tyndale House, 1977.

____ *The Resurrection Factor*. San Bernardino, CA: Here's Life Pub., 1981.

McDowell, Josh, and Don Stewart. *Answers to Tough Questions*. San Bernardino, CA: Here's Life Pub., 1980.

____ *Reasons Why Skeptics Ought to Consider Christianity*. San Bernardino, CA: Here's Life Pub., 1981.

McDowell, Josh, and Bill Wilson. *He Walked Among Us: Evidence for the Historical Jesus*. San Bernardino, CA: Here's Life Pub., 1988.

Montgomery, John Warwick. *Myth, Allegory and Gospel*. Minneapolis, MN: Bethany, 1974.

_____ *The Shape of the Past: A Christian Response to Secular Philosophies of History*. Minneapolis, MN: Bethany, 1975.

_____ "Is Man His Own God?" and other essays in *Christianity for the Tough-Minded*. Minneapolis, MN: Bethany, 1976.

_____ *Evidence for Faith: Deciding the God Question*. Dallas, TX: Probe Books, 1991.

_____ *History and Christianity*.

Moreland, J. P. *Scaling the Secular City*. Grand Rapids, MI: Baker, 1987.

_____ ed. *The Creation Hypothesis: Scientific Evidence for an Intelligent Designer*. Downers Grove, IL: InterVarsity Press, 1995.

Morey, Robert A. *The New Atheism and the Erosion of Freedom*. Minneapolis, MN: Bethany, 1986.

_____ *Introduction to Defending the Faith*.

Morris, Henry M. *The Biblical Basis for Modern Science*. Grand Rapids, MI: Baker, 1984.

Morris, Henry M., with Henry M. Morris, III. *Many Infallible Proofs*. Rev. ed. Green Forest, AR: Master Books, 1996.

Morris, Thomas V. *Making Sense of It All: Pascal and the Meaning of Life*. Grand Rapids, MN: Eerdmans, 1992.

Morrison, Frank. *Who Moved the Stone?* Downers Grove, IL: InterVarsity Press, 1958.

Nash, Ronald H. *Faith and Reason*. Grand Rapids, MI: Zondervan/Academie, 1988.

_____ *Is Jesus the Only Savior?* Grand Rapids, MI: Zondervan, 1994.

Orr, James. *The Christian View of God and the World*. Grand Rapids, MI: Kregel, 1989.

Pache, Rene. *The Inspiration and Authority of Scripture*. Chicago, IL: Moody, 1969.

Packer, J. I. *God Has Spoken*. Downers Grove, IL: InterVarsity Press, 1979.

_____ *Knowing Christianity*. Wheaton, IL: Harold Shaw, 1995.

Parker, Gary. *Dry Bones and Other Fossils*. Green Forest, AR: Master Books, 1985.

_____ *From Evolution to Creation*. San Diego, CA: CLP, 1977.

Pascal, Blaise. *The Thoughts of Blaise Pascal*. Edited by Brunschvicg. Garden City, NY: Doubleday, n.d.

Payne, J. Barton. *Encyclopedia of Biblical Prophecy*. Grand Rapids, MI: Baker, 1989.

Pegis, Anton. *Basic Writings of Saint Thomas Aquinas*. 2 vols. New York, NY: Random House, 1945.

Petersen, Dennis R. *Unlocking the Mysteries of Creation*. Vol. 1. South Lake Tahoe, CA: Christian Equippers International, 1987.

Plantinga, Alvin. *The Ontological Argument*. New York, NY: Anchor Books, 1965.

Prior, Kenneth F. W. *The Gospel in a Pagan society*. Downers Grove, IL: InterVarsity, 1975.

Purtill, Richard L. *Reason to Believe*. Grand Rapids, MI: Eerdmans, 1974.

Radmacher, Earl D., ed. *Can We Trust the Bible?* Wheaton, IL: Tyndale House, 1979.

Ramm, Bernard. *Protestant Christian Evidences*. Chicago, IL: Moody, 1953.

_____ *Varieties of Christian Apologetics*. Grand Rapids, MI: Baker, 1961.

_____ *The God Who Makes A Difference*. Waco, TX: Word, 1972.

_____ *A Christian Appeal to Reason*. Waco, TX: Word, 1972.

Reid, J. K. S. *Christian Apologetics*. Grand Rapids, MI: Eerdmans, 1969.

Reymond, Robert L. *The Justification of Knowledge*. Nutley, NJ: Presbyterian & Reformed, 1976.

Richardson, Don. *Eternity in Their Hearts*. Ventura, CA: Regal, 1981.

Schaeffer, Francis. *Escape from Reason*. Downers Grove, IL: InterVarsity, 1968.

_____ *The God Who Is There*. Downers Grove, IL: InterVarsity, 1968.

_____ *Death in the City*. Downers Grove, IL: InterVarsity, 1969.

_____ *He Is There and He Is Not Silent*. Wheaton, IL: Tyndale, 1972.

Sire, James W. *The Universe Next Door*. 2d ed. Downers Grove, IL: InterVarsity Press, 1988.

_____ *Why Should Anyone Believe Anything at All?* Downers Grove, IL: InterVarsity Press, 1994.

Smith, A. E. Wilder. *Man's Origin, Man's Destiny*. Wheaton, IL: Harold Shaw Pub., 1968.

Smith, Wilbur. *Therefore Stand*. Boston, MA: W. A. Wilde, 1945.

Sproul, R. C. *Basic Training: Plain Talk on the Key Truths of the Faith*. Grand Rapids, MI: Zondervan, 1982.

_____ *If There's a God, Why Are There Atheists?: Why Atheists Believe in Unbelief*. Wheaton, IL: Tyndale, 1996.

_____ *Not a Chance: The Myth of Chance in Modern Science and Cosmology*. Grand Rapids, MI: 1994.

Story, Dan. *Defending Your Faith*. Nashville, TN: Nelson, 1992.

Stott, John R. W. *Basic Christianity*. 2nd ed. Downers Grove, IL: InterVarsity Press, 1971.

Sunderland, Luther. *Darwin's Engima*. Green Forest, AR: Master Books, 1984.

Swinebirne, Richard. *The Concept of Miracle*. New York, NY: St. Martin's, 1970.

_____ *The Existence of God*. Oxford: Clarendon, 1979.

_____ *The Christian God*. Oxford: Clarendon, 1979.

Sylvester, Hugh. *Arguing with God*. Downers Grove, IL: InterVarsity Press, 1971.

Taylor, Paul S. *The Great Dinosaur Mystery and the Bible*. Green Forest, AR: Master Books, 1987.

_____ *The Illustrated Origins Answer Book*. El Cajon, CA: Films for Christ Assn., 1989.

Tenney, Merrill C. *The Reality of the Resurrection*. New York, NY: Harper & Row, 1963.

Thurman, L. Duane. *How to Think about Evolution*. Downers Grove, IL: InterVarsity Press, 1978.

Trueblood, D. Elton. *Philosophy of Religion*. Grand Rapids, MI: Baker, n.d.

Unger, Merrill F. *Archaeology and the Old Testament*. Grand Rapids, MI: Zondervan, 1954.

Van Til, Cornelius. "Apologetics." Unpublished class syllabus, Westminster Theological Seminary, n.d.

_____ *A Christian Theory of Knowledge*. Philadelphia, PA: Presbyterian & Reformed, 1969.

_____ *Defense of the Faith*. Rev. ed. Philadelphia, PA: Presbyterian & Reformed, 1972.

_____ *Jerusalem and Athens*. Edited by E. R. Geehan. Nutley, NJ: Presbyterian & Reformed, 1977.

Vos, Howard. *Can I Trust My Bible?* Chicago, IL: Moody, 1963.

Wenham, John W. *The Goodness of God*. Downers Grove, IL: InterVarsity Press, 1974.

Whitcomb, John C., Jr. *The Early Earth*. Grand Rapids, MI: Baker, 1972.

Wilder-Smith, A. E. *The Creation of Life*. Green Forest, AR: Master Books, 1970.

_____ *God: To Be or Not to Be?* Stuttgart: Telos International, 1975.

_____ *Reliability of the Bible*. Green Forest, AR: Master Books, 1983.

Williams, Rheinallt Nantlais. *Faith, Facts, History, Science — and How They Fit Together*. Wheaton, IL: Tyndale House, 1973.

Wilson, Clifford A. *Rocks, Relics and Biblical Reliability*. Christian Free University Curriculum. Grand Rapids, MI: Zondervan, 1977.

Wolterstorff, Nicholas. *Reason Within the Bounds of Religion*. Grand Rapids, MI: Eerdmans, 1976.

Wood, Barry, *Questions Non-Christians Ask*. Old Tappan, NJ: Revell, 1977.

Wyson, R. L. *The Creation-Evolution Controversy*. Midland, MI: Inquiry Press, 1976.

Yamauchi, Edwin. *The Stones and the Scriptures*. Philadelphia, PA: J. P. Lippincott, 1972.

Yancey, Philip. *Where Is God When It Hurts?* Grand Rapids, MI: Zondervan, 1977.